A woman on the edge of time

A woman on the edge of time

a son's search for his mother

Jeremy Gavron

SCRIBE

Melbourne • London

Scribe Publications
18–20 Edward St, Brunswick, Victoria 3056, Australia
2 John St, Clerkenwell, London, WC1N 2ES, United Kingdom

First published by Scribe in 2015
Reprinted 2015

The author and publishers are grateful to Arnold Wesker for granting permission
to reproduce part of his *Six Days in January*.

The moral right of the author has been asserted.

Typeset in Adobe Caslon Pro 11/16pt by the publishers
Printed and bound in the UK by CPI Group (UK) Ltd, Croydon CR0 4YY

9781925106725 (AU edition)
9781925228090 (UK edition)
9781925113976 (e-book)

CIP records for this title are availab[le from the British Library and the National]
Library of Australia

scribepublications.com.au
scribepublications.co.uk

For Rafi, Benji, Leah, Mosie, and Mima

Have I betrayed them all again by telling the story?

Or is it the other way round:

would I have betrayed them if I had not told it?

Amos Oz

These be the facts

ON PAGE FIVE of its Christmas Eve issue of 1965, among stories of Yuletide parties, the army distributing Christmas cakes, and a shopkeeper charged with receiving stolen long johns, the *Camden & St Pancras Chronicle* of north London ran a brief report on the inquest into the death of a young woman.

The facts, as the reporter laid them out, were straightforward. Ten days earlier, on the afternoon of Tuesday 14 December, Hannah Gavron had dropped the younger of her two sons at a Christmas party at his nursery school in Highgate and driven to a friend's flat in Primrose Hill. There she let herself in, sealed the kitchen door and windows, wrote a brief note, and turned on the gas oven.

A neighbour or perhaps a passing pedestrian must have smelled gas, for a North Thames Gas Board fitter with the unlikely name of Herbert Popjoy was sent to investigate. Obtaining no answer at the front door, he climbed a wall into the back garden, from 'where he saw Mrs Gavron lying by a window'. Forcing his way in, he 'dragged her into the hall and applied the "kiss of life"', but despite his 'heroic efforts' she could not be resuscitated.

The reasons for Mrs Gavron's actions, as reported in the article, were less clear. Her father, Mr Tosco Raphael Fyvel, told the court that his daughter and her husband 'were "going through a difficult

1

phase", but that when he saw her the day before she died she was in an extremely good mood'.

The family's au pair girl, Miss Jean Yvonne Hawes, also testified that the 'last time she saw Mrs Gavron', earlier on the day of her death, 'she was in a very good mood'.

Only Mrs Anne Wicks, the friend in whose flat Mrs Gavron had died, suggested anything different. Mrs Gavron 'had been depressed in the days before her death' and must have 'put on a brave face for her father', she said, though she offered no explanation for Mrs Gavron's state of mind. Nor did she explain why Mrs Gavron had a key to her front door.

Other than a police constable, who found Mrs Gavron's note on a table, and a pathologist from University College Hospital, who stated that the death was due to carbon monoxide poisoning, there were no other witnesses.

Recording a verdict of suicide, the coroner noted that Mrs Gavron's 'marriage had been going through a "sticky phase"', but that this did not seem to account for why 'an academically brilliant, happily employed young woman with a young family should take such a tragic step'. He had presided over more than 1,700 cases of suicide, he said, but never one 'in which the intent to take one's own life had been clearer' and he had been 'so confused about the reason'.

ALL SUICIDES LEAVE some degree of confusion. Suicide is the hardest human act to understand because it challenges the fundamental assumption by which we lead our lives — that life has meaning, value — but also because it leaves no one to explain. Murderers can at least be questioned, but a suicide is a murder in which the killer is also the victim: in which the reason, the motive, dies with the act.

In some cases, factors such as age, illness, financial troubles, loss,

2

provide at least some explanation. Sylvia Plath, who gassed herself two years earlier in a flat one street away from where Hannah Gavron died, had suffered from mental illness since she was a girl and had tried to kill herself before — 'one year in every ten', as she wrote in her poem 'Lazy Lazarus'.

But Hannah's suicide, as the coroner suggested, was particularly confounding. She was twenty-nine, a few months younger than Plath, with two young children, as Plath had had, but she had no history of depression or suicidal impulses. Like Plath, she had been having marital troubles, but whereas Plath was alone with her children in a cold rented flat in a foreign city, Hannah was living in a brand-new house in Highgate, with an au pair girl, surrounded by friendly neighbours, her parents only a few minutes' drive away.

There were things the coroner did not know. When Hannah's father had spoken of her marriage going through a 'difficult phase', what he had not said was that she had been having an affair with a colleague from the art college where she was teaching. The reason she had a key to Anne Wicks's flat was that she had been meeting this man there. In her last days, there had been some kind of argument.

But to those who knew Hannah, the idea that she would kill herself over an affair was hard to accept. 'Inconceivable,' her father wrote in his diary at the time. 'Oh my darling — why, why?' 'Impossible to either grasp or understand,' her friend, Phyllis Willmott, wrote in hers. 'The awful puzzle posed by her act.'

To friends and colleagues, Hannah was a golden girl, an exemplar of what a woman could achieve in the pre-women's-lib days of the mid-1960s. 'There was nobody quite like Hannah,' her fellow sociologist Bernice Martin remembers. 'She was young, attractive, confident, bright, able; she brought an extra jolt to life. To succeed in those days women had to give up something — children, work, femininity —

whereas Hannah wanted and appeared able to have everything.'

She wasn't perhaps conventionally beautiful — her face was too broad, her black hair too bristly, her mouth too big — but with her expressive almond eyes and full lips, which would spread at the slightest provocation into the broadest of smiles, and the life force burning brightly in her, she had always been highly attractive to men. One of the stories told about her was how as a schoolgirl at her progressive boarding school she had had an affair with the headmaster.

Intelligent and poised, she had from a young age been successful in almost everything she did. At eight, another story went, she announced she was going to win a BBC children's poetry competition, and promptly did so. At twelve, she was a champion show-jumper in gymkhanas around southern England. She left school at sixteen to train to be an actress at the Royal Academy of Dramatic Art, where, so the story went, she played in Shakespeare opposite Albert Finney and Peter O'Toole. When she gave up acting and went to London University, she got a first in sociology, and embarked on a PhD, at the same time as having two sons.

While still working on her doctorate, she began reviewing books for *The Economist* and *New Society*. She also started to appear as a pundit on the radio and television. In the last two years of her life, while finishing her thesis and waiting for it to be approved, she was teaching at Hornsey College of Art, one of the epicentres of the heady new world of the Swinging Sixties, which she embraced in her appearance and manner.

'She was a blast of sea air through the place,' David Page, a colleague at Hornsey, remembers. 'I can still see her striding up the corridor: knee-length boots, dark tights and suede mini-skirt, with a Mary Quant hair-do. She would have a cheroot in one hand, a wonderful wide grin, and would quite likely be cursing someone or

4

something. She was the first woman I had met who looked at men the way men traditionally looked at women. She would see a male student passing and say, "I really fancy that one.'"

At the same time, she was a serious sociologist, with a focus on the situation of modern women. In her last months, she had been adapting her doctoral thesis, a study of the conflicts in the lives of young mothers in Kentish Town, into a book. *The Captive Wife*, as she titled it, would prove to be an early statement of the women's movement that was to rise up in the years to follow, and caused something of an uproar when it was published a few months after her death.

But captive wives, unhappy young mothers in north London, women who felt so lonely and desperate that they 'could scream', as she quoted one of her interviewees as saying, were what Hannah wrote about — not what she, with her smart modern house in Highgate, her au pair girl, her job, her book, her knee-length boots, and Mary Quant hair-do, was herself.

HANNAH GAVRON WAS my mother. I am the son she took to nursery school that afternoon in 1965. I was four years old.

This sense of my mother as two different people — the attractive, brilliant, free-spirited Hannah who lived her life to the full, and the Hannah who mysteriously decided she couldn't go on living at all — was what I grew up with.

I wasn't told this any of this directly. After her death, my father decided that it was better if we didn't talk about her. I don't remember much about those first couple of years after her death, but once my father had remarried and our new family began to expand, we moved house; and though I lived in our new home until I left at eighteen, I don't remember Hannah ever being mentioned under its roof. Nor were there any photographs of her on display, or any other sign of her,

5

except for a few copies of *The Captive Wife*, up on a high shelf, where other parents might have kept books by Henry Miller or Anaïs Nin.

My grandparents, Hannah's parents, did have a few pictures of her on the wall in their house in Primrose Hill (barely a hundred yards from where she died, though it wasn't until much later that I learned this). My grandmother was also the one person who talked to me about her — or at least repeated the same handful of stories about her youthful mischiefs and adventures. How she locked the housekeeper in the chicken shed until she promised to stop smacking her son. How she dropped a penny on the bus so she could bend down and look up a Scotsman's kilt to see 'the thing itself'. How she wanted to marry my father at seventeen, but my grandparents made her wait until she was eighteen.

By then my own memories of her had long vanished. It was partly the age I was when she died — we don't start to prioritise autobiographical memory until we are about five. But I have a clear memory of the morning after her death, my father sitting my brother and me down on the end of his bed to tell us. I remember the knowledge of her absence, too. When I grew up and learned about phantom limbs, how an amputated arm or leg can still produce sensation, I understood how this must feel. But when I try to look back to her I see only blackness.

My father spoke to me about her only once in the years I lived at home. It was the summer after my sixteenth birthday. We were in his car — I don't remember where we were going, and perhaps we were driving for the purpose of this conversation, for sitting side by side as we were he did not have to look at me. After her death he had told my brother and me that she had died of a heart attack, but now he told me a different story. He had never stopped loving her, he said, but she had fallen for a colleague who turned out to be homosexual, and when this man rejected her she felt she had messed things up and killed herself.

I remember my eyes blurring, and wondering if I wanted my father to see that I was crying. Beyond that, I didn't know what to think or feel. I don't remember asking any questions or wondering if there might be more to the story than he had told me.

My interest in her must have been stirred, for as well as the copies of her book, which I already knew about, I found a couple of other things. One was a bag of rosettes and cups I realised must have been hers from her showjumping. I polished up a couple of the larger cups and put them on a shelf in my bedroom.

The other was a box of old photographs. I have it beside me now, and there are pictures in it of Hannah with me, though the one I chose to take was a portrait of her as a teenager — a headshot, I now realise, from her time at acting school. She would have been seventeen or possibly eighteen, not much older than I was, but with her carefully coiffed hair, a silk scarf knotted around her neck, her eyes gazing away from the camera, she seemed to me impossibly sophisticated and glamorous. Written in a corner in looping letters (the first of her handwriting I had ever seen) were the words, 'Bewitched, bothered and bewildered, but always yours', which I guessed must have been for my father, but I fantasised were for me, and for a while I was a little in love with the girl in that photograph.

I put her up in my room alongside the cups. I hadn't talked to anyone about what my father had told me, and perhaps I hoped that he or my brother or my stepmother might comment on these artefacts, that this might lead to more talk about Hannah, though as far as I remember no one said anything.

Soon, anyway, I was leaving home to go to university, and I spent the rest of my twenties working as a journalist in Africa and Asia, too wrapped up in my own present to worry much about the past. It wasn't

7

until I came back to London at the age of twenty-nine — the age she was when she died — that my thoughts turned to her again and I learned more about her and her death.

My grandfather had died, and we decided to move my grandmother, who was suffering from dementia, into sheltered accommodation. Helping my aunt Susie, Hannah's sister, sort through the house in Primrose Hill, I found three items.

The first was a yellowed cutting of the article from the *Camden & St Pancras Chronicle*. From this I learned the facts of Hannah's death, including the date and the place where she died, as well as about her dropping me at the Christmas party.

The second was her suicide note. No one had ever told me that she had left a note, but I understood immediately that this is what it was. It was written in large, untidy letters across both sides of a small white envelope. There were thirty-three words in all — four more than the years of her life. Several were taken up with an apology to Anne Wicks. At the bottom of the first side was written 'P.T.O.', as if whoever found the note might not think to turn it over. Scrawled diagonally across the back were the words, 'Please tell the boys I did love them terribly!'

I remember showing the note to Susie, and how she shuddered and turned away. I remember, too, the third item — my grandfather's diary from the last months of Hannah's life. I turned the pages until I came to the day of Hannah's death. But the words I began to read were too graphic, the pain on the page too raw — I didn't know my mother, but I had known and loved my grandfather — and I dropped the diary back into the box where I had found it.

I did, though, take away the newspaper article and the envelope — and some time afterwards I brought up Hannah's death with my father. We were walking on Hampstead Heath — side by side, it strikes me now, as we were in the car. I remember him stiffening beside me, and the dull feeling that settled on me when I realised that he wasn't going to say much more than he had told me at sixteen, though also my relief when the conversation was over, that I could breathe again.

I didn't say anything about the note, but perhaps I mentioned the newspaper article, and what Anne Wicks had said to the inquest about Hannah being depressed, for he told me that Hannah had been to see a psychiatrist before her death. My grandmother had encouraged her to do so, but the 'eminent psychiatrist' she consulted had 'told her that there was nothing wrong with her'.

He also spoke with a bitterness that shocked me about Anne Wicks, saying she had influenced Hannah against him, though he didn't explain any further and I didn't ask for more details.

I was thirty years old, had been a journalist for six years, had recently published my first book — an investigation into the mysterious death of a young woman in Africa. There were things I could easily have done to learn more about Hannah. I could have tracked down Anne Wicks and got her side of the story. I could have asked Susie for the boxes of my grandfather's diaries and read them. I could have talked to my brother, who had told me once that he remembered Hannah, could have asked him for his son's-eye view of her, but I didn't — as I didn't show him the article, as I never told him about her note, never shared with him the message she had left for us.

Spring 1952

Cher Tash, I am sick of French I already almost dream in it, but to be quite honest I dont think I will improve much, if people talk slowly I understand pretty well but you would be surprised how silent I am I hardly say anything.

This isnt a school at all, and there are no other children here but me. At first I was terribly lonely at the thought of spending three weeks without company of my own age, but now I don't mind nearly so much, but I certainly miss male company, do you know I haven't spoken to a young boy for over two weeks, and the French boys are _so_ attractive — its _most_ frustrating!

Monsieur is a funny old chap — he reminds me of a walrus — he has a large moustache which he combs with a little pink comb! he cracks jokes all the time — feeble ones at that, half of which I dont understand, but I just laugh when he stops and thats ok.

I have the most wonderful view from my window, out across the Seine, over the Bois de Boulogne straight to the Eiffel Tower, and a little to the left is the Arc de Triomphe. The Bois de Boulogne is beautiful. _If_ I ever get married I shall cart my fiancee here and make him walk through it with me.

Coming over on the plane I had an affair with a man of about 30, who is the personal assistant to Lord Beaverbrook, and works on the Express. He bought me some brandy, and a cup of coffee, and invited me to go to St Tropez with him — I was very tempted. He gave me his card and said that he was always in Paris and I was to ring him at the offices of the Express and he would take me out for dinner! You know I rather think I will!

10

Madame raised her eyebrows when I told her that I went to a mixed boarding school, they consider me a little innocent nevertheless! — little do they know!!!!

One

IT IS THE last day of March 2005, and I am driving with my wife and two daughters, aged nine and seven, down to the Sussex coast. We are heading to the barn my father bought when I was about nine myself, shortly after the second of my half sisters was born, as a holiday home for our new family.

As we leave the city, I get that familiar feeling of shedding troubles and responsibilities, that the trees and hills can renew me. Driving through the Downs, I have an urge to stop and follow one of the footpath signs pointing across a field or into a shadowy wood. But we only have three days away — I need to be back in London next week for the publication of my new novel — and the girls are eager to get to the Barn. I left my phone at home, and when we set out I suggested Judy turns hers off, too. Visits to the Barn are a chance to escape the call of the electronic world. For the next three days we will fish for crabs in the tidal pools on the beach, and play charades in front of the fire.

When we arrive, we unpack the car, and while Judy drives off to the village to shop, the girls and I open up the bike shed. We share the Barn with my brother's and my sisters' families, and I am irritated to see that some of the bikes have flat tyres. I find two that will do for Leah and Jemima; they take them off to ride on the tennis court, and I wheel a couple of others out onto the grass to fix them.

The sun is shining, and my annoyance soon ebbs. I am happy to be here — happy that the girls are outside riding bikes, happy to be doing something with my hands rather than my mind. I fetch the bike tools and a bucket of water, and use the tyre levers to free the first tyre from the rim. I find the puncture, but when I open the repair box the glue has hardened. I go inside to find another kit. As I turn to walk back out, I notice a red light blinking on the phone.

It is probably an old message, probably nothing to do with us, but it is hard to ignore, and I walk over and press the button and hear my father's voice — or rather a strangely crumpled, strangely affected, version of his voice.

My first reaction is embarrassment that he should be speaking like this, should be expressing his emotions so unnaturally. Though even as I am thinking this I am taking in what he is saying. 'The worst news,' are his words. 'Call me.'

I glance instinctively out into the garden in search of my daughters. The worst news would be something happening to them. I cannot see them, but I can hear their cheerful voices as they ride around the tennis court.

By now, though, I understand that this is serious. The worst news must mean — and though I do not allow myself to finish this thought, a roulette wheel is turning in my head as I dial my father's number.

Normally it would be my father, who is in his mid-seventies, who has had two heart bypasses, I would be worried about, but it can't be him.

Perhaps, I think, it is his brother, who also has heart problems, though before the idea is halfway through my mind I know it is not.

'Dad?' I say, when he answers the phone.

'Simon' is the name he utters, that his words fall on. Not my

14

daughters — his son. Not his brother — my brother.

A seizure, I hear him say — Simon has suffered from seizures in the past. Earlier this morning, he says. His body was found in the street near his house.

When I have put down the phone, I stand in the watery air. How long has it been since I came in to look for the glue? A minute? Two?

What I am aware of feeling at this moment is not shock or grief or even disbelief, so much as a lack of interest in what I've heard. I do not want to know this information. What has it got to do with our weekend at the Barn? I want to continue the day as we have planned, for Judy to return with the shopping, for us all to cycle down to the beach. The sun is still shining outside, after all. No one has died down here.

Although I have told my father we will head back to London straight away, I walk out into the garden with the glue. Judy won't be back with the car for a while, and I have a job to do here, a task to finish. I have marked the puncture spot, and I find the hole and rub it down and smooth a circle of glue over it.

I don't remember much about the journey back except that I insist we stop to buy sandwiches, and that everyone gets what they want, even if it means going to two different shops. I remember, too, Judy saying at some point that at least my family knows how to deal with death, and looking at her in surprise.

At my father's house, we learn what happened. Playing football the previous evening, Simon felt what he thought was indigestion, and when the pain was still there in the morning he went out to run it off. An hour later, a policewoman rang on his door. His wife had to stay with the two younger boys, and his oldest son, Rafi, who is fifteen, volunteered to go the hospital to identify his father.

15

I ask if anyone else has seen the body, and when they say no, I say that I want to go. I am not sure why I am so insistent, but I am almost giddy at the thought. Perhaps I think that as Rafi has seen him, I must, too, that I can take the burden of what he has witnessed from him. Perhaps it is simply that I need to do something, though later it will occur to me that I needed to see Simon for myself — needed the knowledge of seeing his body, the evidence, the truth.

Simon's wife and boys have been at my father's house, but they are back home now, and Judy wants to go to them. On the way she drops me at the hospital. I am familiar with this place — both my girls were born here, I have had my own head stitched up here — but where a nurse now takes me is further back than I have been before, further back than I imagined the building goes, through doors with no entry signs on them, down hallways where patients do not go.

I wait outside while the nurse prepares him. When she calls me in, he is lying on the bed, his arms crossed on his belly. I am surprised to see him in a hospital gown. I had imagined him still wearing his jogging clothes.

'You can touch him if you want,' the nurse says, lifting one of his hands and letting it flop down again to show me how it is done.

I have seen death before. As a young journalist in Africa I walked through a meadow of bodies — a hundred rebel soldiers cut down by the Ugandan army, young men and women, their skin punctured with bullet holes. But this is different. This is not a nameless body, not a story. This is my brother.

The nurse asks if I want to be alone with him, and I nod and she bustles away. I move forward to the side of the bed. I both can see that he is dead and do not entirely believe it. His skin is waxy, lifeless, but one eye is slightly ajar, and a sliver of blue iris gazes upwards.

I am not used to being so close to him. When we were boys, if I

16

came this near I was likely to be clouted. The story, the explanation, I have heard, that Simon told me once himself, is that Hannah was too young when she had him, that she found it easier to love me when I came along, and this is what lay between us. I am not sure I believe this either, but for as long as I remember, Simon and I have been wary of each other, and though as adults we eventually found a way to be friends of a sort, I have never entirely lost my fear of him, his strength, his anger.

And now I stand over him and look down at his handsome face. His curls have fallen back from his brow, and I see how far his hair has receded, how he must have cultivated these curls to fall over his forehead. And though I am still afraid of him, I pick up his hand the way the nurse showed me.

While my sisters and sister-in-law gather each day to work out the arrangements for the funeral and to comfort each other, I cannot sit still — I am filled with energy, a sense of purpose. Later, I will realise this is adrenalin, crisis arousal, though now I wonder if it is what it is like to be the oldest, as I am now.

My most urgent conviction is that we must lose no time in saving memories of Simon. I come up with the idea of collecting words and phrases that describe him or that we associate with him, and I call family and friends for suggestions, and type them up for the funeral handout. I drive to my daughters' school to borrow a couple of easels so that people can write down more words or memories at the funeral. I send out emails asking for longer contributions to a memory bank.

But when it comes to the funeral itself, while my sisters, my stepmother, and several of Simon's friends make eloquent, moving speeches, and tell funny stories about him, what I say when I stand up to speak is barely coherent, even though I am the writer in the

17

family, the storyteller. It is partly that my feelings about Simon are so confused. But it also comes from the understanding that once a life has been turned into stories it becomes those stories, and I am not ready for that.

In the weeks that follow, my restlessness gives way to other moods and feelings. I try to comfort Simon's boys, to be with them, but it is awkward between us. In time we will become close, but for now I am, I suppose, too much like Simon and not enough — some strange half-ghost of their father.

Now that we are supposed to be resuming our lives, the disbelief comes. As a child, I dreamed that my mother was not really dead, that she would eventually come back, and now, walking along the street, standing in queues, I see Simon ahead of me and have to resist the temptation to call his name. The morning after his death, I turned on my computer and there was an email from him, a message from the grave, and now I see coded messages about him in car number plates, in advertisement hoardings. Everything reminds me of him.

There are episodes of happiness, exhilaration — chemical compensations of the brain, perhaps — though I entertain guilty thoughts, too, which I do not admit to anyone, that I have won, that by outlasting Simon I have emerged the triumphant brother in some competition extending from our childhood.

Though, more and more, what I feel is a tremendous grief, a sorrow that catches me five, ten times a day, and sets me sobbing helplessly.

A couple of weeks after the funeral, the whole family goes to see Simon's middle son, Benji, play in a football cup final. When Benji's side win, when they are presented with the cup, the others cheer and clap, but I cannot look, am turned to the wall, my body heaving, my eyes blind with tears.

I am grateful for this, grateful that, for all my guilty thoughts, my confusion, I am able to mourn Simon, though I am also unnerved by the force of these emotions. I am a natural sceptic, suspicious of what I cannot see to be true, but in the face of so much feeling I am carried into unfamiliar territory. I do not doubt that I am grieving for Simon, for his boys, for all the things I didn't say to him, that I will never now say. But these tides of grief feel so elemental, seem to be welling up from some place so deep inside me, that I come to wonder whether Simon's death has not also dislodged an older grief in me, the way an earthquake might open a crack in the ground and expose something long buried.

It turns out, once the autopsy is conducted, that Simon probably died of a heart attack, that the seizure was a secondary product of a cardiac event. The discomfort he felt playing football was chest pain. I was supposed to have been playing in that evening football game — one of the few things Simon and I did together. But instead I was giving an interview to a journalist about my novel, and afterwards I am haunted by the thought that if I had been at the game I would have suspected that the pain might be his heart, would have insisted he go to hospital.

For a long time, I cannot write. I find it hard even to read. Words seem to me untrustworthy things; all stories to lead to the same end.

As a family, we do not erase Simon from our lives as we did with Hannah. We talk about him to his boys. We put up pictures of him on our walls and a stone for him in Highgate cemetery, engraved with some of the words and phrases we collected for his funeral. We gather each year on the anniversary of his death. The first year, my aunt Susie's husband, the only one among us who knows any prayers, says kaddish, the Jewish prayer for the dead. But he never does this again, and each year we mention Simon less, are less inclined to share memories of him. It is easier not to think, to close one's mind and move on.

At the same time, what was unearthed in me to do with Hannah remains exposed. She has always been present in some corner of my mind; but, since having my daughters, the first girls to be born in the family since her death, I have thought more about her. When Leah was four she looked uncannily like a photograph of Hannah I had found in my grandparents' house, and I put this up in our kitchen and was delighted when people mistook it for Leah. But I still found it hard to talk about Hannah, her death. When, a year or two before, Leah asked how Hannah died, I panicked. I didn't want to lie to her, but neither did I want to burden her with the truth. I put her off for several months, though when I finally told her, she said, 'Oh, I thought she was murdered,' and walked off to play.

Now, though I don't talk to my family, I find myself blurting out about her suicide to people I hardly know, cornering strangers like the ancient mariner, or Conrad's Marlow, with my inconclusive story.

I am almost exactly the age Simon was when he died, playing in the same weekly football game, when I have a cardiac event of my own. Like Simon, I begin to feel unwell during the game. I have a slight ear infection, and I tell myself it is my ear, that I will go to the doctor tomorrow to get antibiotics, and I continue playing. But when the game ends I am still conscious of a pressure on my chest, and I take myself to the hospital. It is a heart attack, but caught early, and fortunately a small one. The cardiologist threads three stents into my arteries, and within a few weeks I am back to running and playing football.

The symmetry of what has happened is not lost on me. I have survived in part because of what happened to Simon. If it wasn't for his death I probably wouldn't have gone to the hospital. I might have woken the next morning, gone for a walk or a run as he did, and ended up in a different part of the building.

It is common after a heart attack to be depressed, but I feel invigorated, re-engaged with life. We throw a party. I delight in telling people what has happened, how I have beaten the family curse, have not died young.

Within a few months, I complete my first proper piece of writing since Simon died, and I begin working on a new novel, an idea about an unexplained death I have had in my mind for a long time, though now I see it from the point of view of a journalist investigating the case. But while I know how the story should feel — part fairy tale, part detective story, magical and ordinary at the same time — I cannot get this feeling to come to life on the page, as if there is still a disconnect between my emotions and my intellect, my heart and my head.

Six months after my heart attack, leafing through a newspaper, I come upon an article about the recent suicide of Nicholas Hughes, the son of Ted Hughes and Sylvia Plath. I have long known that there were similarities between Plath's death and my mother's, but what I read now sends a chill of recognition through me. It is not only the proximity of the two flats, the ages of the two women, the gas ovens. Nicholas Hughes was forty-seven, as I am. Like my father, Ted Hughes apparently tried to keep the truth from his children until they were older. Like me, the article suggests, Nicholas Hughes was deeply affected by a second death — in his case, that of his father.

By the time I have finished reading, I know I am going to write something about Hannah. I call the *Guardian* and all but insist that the editor I speak to commissions the piece, which I write in a state of nervous exhilaration, the words flowing from me, and I file straight away, so that I cannot change my mind.

Summer — autumn 1953

Dear Tash, I am madly jealous, you seem to be having a wonderful time and you must be getting so brown. I am helping in a theatre club in Shaftsbury Avenue. Actually not half as exciting as it sounds because they have only just moved in and the stage is not up yet, so they can't do any plays, I have been helping get things straight and also served behind the bar!!

I have been playing masses of tennis with a really sweet Israeli boy called Mike. The only difficulty is keeping him at the proper distance. I also went down with him to stay at the sea in Kent for a few days with some relatives of Shirley which was lovely we tore about madly in a cronky old car. I am probably going there again for three days tomorrow. Mummy and Daddy are off tomorrow and refuse to let me stay alone in the flat.

Do you know K called in to see me a couple of weeks ago — just walked in I got a heck of a shock — he stayed for lunch too! Dear K I wonder what Mum and Daddy thought. His letter arrived while I was at the sea & Mum rang up and said should she open it because it was sure to be my results. I of course said NO.

Dear Tash, You ask about the party. Well personally I don't enjoy them, although this was certainly better than most! Sonia looked wonderful and I hired myself a very pretty costume. I got pally with a boy in a Spanish costume who looked ravishing and who I discovered was also going on the stage. However when he took his mask off he was quite ordinary & the look in his eye spelt one thing only — necking — so I gave him the cold shoulder.

Do find out my marks sometime & look after K. He is much nicer than one imagines in the hols. I have had a nice letter from Mike — I miss him at odd moments its a case of wishing he was here but not being miserable because he isn't.

Dear Tash, I have at last found a girl in my class who is really very nice. Its such a relief to find someone who knows that the reason why the man who takes us for makeup is so very charming and full of little jokes is because he is as 'queer' as a coot!

Dear Tash, How did seeing C work out? — honestly Tash I know it's none of my business but I should avoid seeing him too often — you might just as well learn how to do without each other for fairly long periods — oh heck its your life not mine I probably dont know what I am talking about!

I wrote to K, and told him to think of me sometimes when he is working in his study with the door open — I wonder if he does. Its highly unlikely!! I miss him like hell sometimes, and if you know what I mean I am conscious of him in most things I do.

Two

WHAT I WRITE for the *Guardian* is as much about what I don't know as what I do, about living in the shadow of suicide as about Hannah herself, but waiting for it to be published I am more anxious than I have ever been over a book. With a book, my worries are about reviews and sales, whether readers will like it — not that the sky might fall in, that what I have written might finish off my father.

I spoke to him while I was writing it, and though he told me I must do what I needed to do, I could hear him stiffening down the line, as he had on our walk on Hampstead Heath a dozen years before. If there are two Hannahs, there are also two of my father: the confident, commanding patriarch he usually is, and the halting, almost wordless person he becomes when Hannah is mentioned.

Even in my earliest memories, there was something of the chief executive officer about my father, but he wasn't distant from Simon and me. He would get down on the carpet in his bedroom to play with us. At bedtime, he read me books like *The Wind in the Willows*, or told me stories he made up.

As I grew older, he came to watch me play sport for my school, standing on the touchline on cold, wet afternoons. For years, he took me for a walk every Sunday morning across Hampstead Heath. I don't remember any particular conversations, but I can see us in my mind's eye, my father asking about school, books I was reading, my sports teams, or trying to interest me in his world.

Nor was our house a furtive or unhappy place, at least until his marriage to my stepmother began to fall apart a decade later. New life soon came along in the shape of my half-sisters, and my stepmother, young and hippyish, devoted herself to us. More than twenty years after their divorce, she still likes to tell the story of how my father courted her. He wanted to be home in the evenings to put Simon and me to bed, so he took her for tea at the Ritz. He had bought a business in the last couple of years of Hannah's life, had gone out on his own and taken on debts, and he told her he wasn't sure his heart was in it. He talked of selling up, buying a boat, sailing around the world, starting a new life.

It was, my stepmother says, partly why she married him, though he never bought that boat. Instead he carried on with his business, forging it into a success, as we carried on with our family life, holding to the same course we had been on before Hannah's death, only with a different mother, the old one unmentioned, almost as if she had never existed.

THE NIGHT BEFORE the article is due out, I can't sleep, and I get up early and walk down to the newsagent. Opening the newspaper in the street to see the headline, a photograph of Hannah holding me, my hands start shaking, and I glance around, but the street is empty: no one is staring at me.

As the morning goes on, the phone rings, emails start to arrive — none suggesting I have done anything terrible. My aunt Susie calls, pledging to try to break 'the old pattern of silence'. Simon's wife emails with a memory of Simon telling her about Hannah when they first met, warning her that he wasn't a good bet. He would have appreciated

26

the article, she writes, though I am not sure I could have written it if he was still alive. My father calls to say that several people have spoken to him positively about the article. His voice is a little easier, and I wonder if an old weight might not have lifted a little from him, too.

Letters also come, from family friends, from strangers to me who write that they knew Hannah. One is from a woman who recalls Hannah coming to her sister's fancy-dress party as 'a ravishing Carmen (with a large flower in her hair) aged, oh, maybe 17 or 18. I remember how vivacious and beautiful she was.' Another is the letter in which David Page, Hannah's colleague at Hornsey College of Art, writes of her striding the corridors and fancying the students. 'She was a wonderful vivid person, one of those you never forget. I'm really sorry you never had the chance to know her as an adult, the way we knew her.'

This letter makes me smile, and I keep it out to show to people, read it again and again. I write to David to thank him, and it is not until several weeks have passed that it occurs to me that I could ask him if he has more memories of her. It is an obvious thought — but to me it is a lightning bolt. It is engrained in me that we do not talk about Hannah in my family. But then David Page is not my family.

I send him an email, but he writes back to say he that does not think he has much more to tell me. I try the woman who wrote of Hannah as Carmen, but she only met Hannah that one time. I am disappointed, but something has shifted in my mind, and I think about who else I could try.

The obvious people are two sisters, Sonia and Tasha Edelman, childhood friends of Hannah's, who figured in my grandmother's stories. I have met Tasha, and have an added reason to want to see her. Some years ago, I learned from Susie that Tasha had some letters from Hannah, though when I called Tasha she said she had lost them. But

27

Susie tells me now that Tasha's health, which has been bad for some time, has worsened. She has had a stroke, and barely talks. She suggests instead that I write to Sonia.

While I am waiting for a reply, I email an old neighbour of ours from Hannah's time. Deborah Van der Beek — Kartun as she was — is only a few years older than me, but I hope she might be able to give me something of the child's view of Hannah I never got from Simon and have lost in myself.

Deborah replies immediately, and a couple of days later I drive to Wiltshire to see her and her mother, who lives nearby. Deborah is an artist, and lives in a beautifully restored Queen Anne vicarage with a walled garden full of her sculptures; but, walking around with her, I find it hard to take anything in, and it is a relief when we sit down to talk about Hannah.

Deborah's family were the first to move into the modern development in Highgate where we lived next door to each other, she tells me, and we were the second. Her parents were quite a bit older than mine, but they soon became good enough friends to go away together. Deborah talks about a holiday in the New Forest, when Hannah took her riding in the frost, and another in the south of France, when she remembers my parents dressing up to go dancing in St Tropez, Hannah in 'fitting slacks with foot straps, looking glamorous, laughing', and my father 'clearly terribly proud of her beauty and vibrancy'.

Hannah was almost young enough to be Deborah's big sister, and she remembers her skipping and playing hula-hoop with her in the garden. She was fascinated by Hannah, she says, how 'pretty and vivacious' she was, how she could be 'feminine, but also tomboyish'. The families sometimes shared the school run, and Deborah talks of being in Hannah's car, a little Fiat, when she drove along the pavement to get around traffic — one of my grandmother's stories.

Later, we drive to the next village to see her mother. Gwen begins by saying how clearly she remembers Hannah, what a 'terrific sense of humour' she had, how attractive and genuine she was, 'down to earth, not phony at all'. But when I press her for more details, her eyes grow misty. She is in her late eighties, and the times we are talking about are half a century ago.

The only specific memory she can come up with is of the weekend before Hannah's death. She and her husband had flown to Paris, leaving Deborah and her sister with the au pair girl, but the night they were due back there was fog at Orly airport, and the planes were grounded.

When Gwen called home to say they were having to stay another night in Paris, the au pair told her that Mrs Gavron had telephoned. If she had known, if she had had any idea, she would have phoned Hannah immediately, she says. But she didn't know, how could she have known? — she didn't even know that my parents' marriage was in difficulties. A year or two earlier, we had moved to another, slightly larger house in the same development, and though it was only around the corner, she hadn't seen so much of Hannah.

'I didn't know she was depressive,' she says.

'She was depressive?'

'Well, she must have been, mustn't she?' she says. 'To do what she did.'

A COUPLE OF DAYS later, I take the train down to Bristol to see Sonia Edelman, or Jackson as she is now. Staring out of the train window, I am excited, nervous, as if I am going on an assignation. The Kartuns were friends, neighbours, but Sonia was Hannah's childhood intimate — the possessor, surely, of some deeper knowledge.

Sonia has offered to meet me at the station, and when I walk out, the first thing she says is, 'You look like Hannah.' I feel myself blushing.

29

It is the first time anyone has ever told me I look like my mother.

Sonia herself is handsome, her hair still blonde, though I am taken aback by how old she is. I always think of Hannah as young, never more than twenty-nine, but Sonia is in her seventies. Glancing at her as she walks to the car, trying to imagine Hannah this age, is like trying to imagine a fairy-tale princess as a grandmother.

In the car, Sonia starts talking in a rush about Hannah, their childhoods in the Buckinghamshire countryside, her own family. 'But you know this,' she keeps saying, and I have to keep telling her that I don't, that all I know is that during the war Hannah lived in a cottage on the edge of Amersham, that it was here she locked the housekeeper in the chicken shed.

Hannah and my grandparents moved to Amersham in 1942, Sonia thinks, when Hannah was six. The Edelmans were already living in a big house with a tennis court a couple of miles away in posher Chesham Bois — Sonia's father, Maurice Edelman, was a novelist and Labour member of parliament.

Hannah often came to stay. They had a group of friends who lived around Chesham Bois, with whom they would go riding. Amersham still had a squire in those days, and his wife took a particular interest in Hannah and let her keep her pony in their stables. I ask why, and Sonia looks at me if I am being deliberately obtuse. 'Because Hannah was so charming and attractive and beautiful, of course,' she says. 'Not like the average child at all. And a wonderful rider.'

Sonia and Tasha also competed at the pony club meetings, but it was Hannah who 'won everything', though on the rare occasions she lost there would be 'floods of tears', and she would need 'lots of calming down'.

Sonia was the older, but Hannah was the leader. She remembers a holiday to Bexhill. Hannah took out a rowing boat and managed it perfectly, but when Sonia and Tasha took out a boat, they drifted out to sea and had to be rescued.

When Hannah went off to board at Frensham Heights in Surrey, Tasha insisted on following her. Sonia was already at another school, but she remembers going with her parents to Frensham and seeing Hannah in a production of *The Duchess of Malfi*, in which 'she was brilliant, naturally'.

She talks of another boating holiday, when they were fifteen or sixteen, to Sweden, run by a man who had sailed with Shackleton. She and Tasha had been with the same group to Holland a year earlier, and Hannah was the newcomer, but she made herself the centre of attention by 'picking on this rather ordinary boy and deciding to have a passionate affair with him'.

Hannah was 'notorious for always wanting to be in love with some boy'. She was 'always creating dramas around herself'.

She talks about Hannah and my father, who met when she was seventeen and he was twenty-three, 'how completely wrapped up in each other they were'.

She didn't see so much of Hannah after she was married. The last time they met was when Hannah was interviewing women for *The Captive Wife*, which must have been a couple of years before her death.

I ask about Hannah's suicide, and she says she always assumed it was 'a dramatic gesture', that she hadn't meant to kill herself. Someone had told her that she was expecting the woman whose flat it was to come back. Though she says also that she didn't think 'Hannah would have liked ageing. I don't see her having a happy life.'

Hannah wasn't 'prone to depression', she says, but she did have 'fits of despair if things didn't go her way'. She didn't like 'having to compromise'.

'The thing about Hannah,' she says, 'is that you were always interested in her. You were never bored with Hannah.'

LATER, AT HOME, I stand at the mirror. I have taken pride in my daughter's resemblance to Hannah, but it is only now, after Sonia's words at the train station, that it occurs to me to look for my mother in my own face, to reach up and touch my broad jaw, run my finger along my full lips.

These meetings with the Kartuns and Sonia have left me in an uncertain state. It is only a couple of weeks since I had the idea of writing to David Page in the hope of hearing some more charming stories about Hannah, but in that time my expectations have both risen and been dampened.

When Sonia talked about Hannah I could tell that she saw her vividly in her own mind, was remembering a whole world; but without any memories of Hannah myself, her memories are only words, stories.

At the same time, I am not sure how much I liked some of what she told me: about Hannah being a poor loser, her need to be the centre of attention, how she was notorious for having to be in love with someone or other. Do I really want to know that Hannah wasn't always such a magical figure?

What Sonia said about Hannah not wanting to grow old also bothers me. What about Simon and me? I want to ask her. Wouldn't she have wanted to see us grow up? Though, do I really want to know the answer? I am old enough to be my mother's father, but I am her son, and children never stop wanting their parents' love, never lose their ability to be hurt by them.

I AM STILL turning all this over in my head when I go to lunch at my father's. I make a point of telling him what I have been doing, who I have been seeing, but he doesn't ask about these meetings, and talks instead about Deborah's father, Derek, who is dead, and about how so many of his friends are dead.

Later, though, to my surprise, he makes a suggestion. I am about to go with my wife and daughters to Israel to see my sister, whose husband has been posted there by the BBC, and her family. While I am there, he says, I should look up his cousin Shirley, who was Hannah's friend, who was with her at Frensham Heights. It may even have been through Shirley, now he thinks of it, that he took up with Hannah.

I haven't seen Shirley since I was a child myself, but I write to her, and a week later we are sitting in the sunshine in my sister's Jerusalem garden.

While Shirley talks, I look through some photographs she has brought along. The pictures of Hannah I have seen before are either as a young girl or after she met my father. But these are from Hannah's boarding-school days, and show a puppyish teenager. In one, she is sitting in a voluminous skirt on a motor cycle; in another, she is standing, legs splayed, in the snow; in a third, she is peeking round a post box. In all three, she has a big grin on her face.

'Han', Shirley calls her — a shortening I have never heard before. 'You can resent another child who shines as brightly as Han did,' Shirley says, 'but I never resented her. She was so terribly attractive, so full of life, with this wide smile that took up her whole face like the Cheshire cat.'

She has a vivid memory of Hannah at a school dance. Hannah had this boyfriend — 'Robert something foreign'. She remembers him coming up behind Hannah, wrapping his arms around her. Hannah was wearing a yellow 1950s dress that was tight at the waist and flared out below, and Shirley can still see it billowing out as this boy put his arms around her.

33

'That's the dress, there,' she says, pointing to another photograph. It is of a group of young people sitting in formal wear around a table. Shirley is in it, and my father, looking ridiculously young, and Hannah in the centre of the picture. She has turned in her chair to look at the photographer. Her face is smooth and round, she is still only seventeen, but there is a look on it, a mixture of innocence and knowingness, that draws me to it, makes me curious about her in a way I have never felt before.

Shirley is telling a story about staying the night at my father's parents' house with Hannah and my father, and there being shenanigans with the bedrooms, but I am only half listening. These photographs, this talk of Frensham Heights, this look on Hannah's face, has raised something else in my mind — the story of Hannah's 'affair' with her headmaster.

I have never properly questioned this word before, have always imagined a precocious fifteen-year-old Hannah seducing a bumbling middle-aged man. I heard from somewhere that he lost his job, and I have always felt faintly sorry for him, as if he was another victim of Hannah's impetuosity, like the housekeeper in the chicken shed. But now, suddenly, I want to know more.

When I ask, Shirley's smiling face sours. 'K,' she says, almost spitting out the name. Hannah didn't seduce him, she says — he seduced her. He wrote her letters, chased her up to London. My father found the letters at some point and showed them to my grandparents, and they took them to the school and he was fired. 'Apparently,' she says, 'he'd done it before.'

Autumn 1953

Dear Tash, I am very sorry to hear that you are ill. That must be why you seemed so gloomy on Sunday. I must confess I was very worried about you, you seemed jolly fed up.

K — he is a darling I'm afraid he must have been rather sad that I hardly saw him. He wanted me to come into his study, but my courage failed me and I made an excuse and ran away. There's so much I would like to say to him, but I felt shy, and I'm jolly well never writing to him again. When you are well and back in circulation please give him my love and say I'm very sorry that I didn't really have time to see him for long.

I'm terribly busy, but its funny how when one is in a crowd of people or rushing around madly one can be very lonely. I miss K and you terribly sometimes. K idealised me so much, but it certainly was comforting to have him believing so utterly in me. There are times when I'd give anything to talk to him.

We are doing a childrens show to take to four different schools. Well it has been cast and I am a fox, a blind mouse, a sheep, a frog, a dwarf (Grumpy!) and the Gryphon (from Alice.) It really is great fun.

We had a stupid discussion in Voice Prod, about knowing oneself, and it got frightfully religious, so I stood up and said firmly that I didnt believe in God, there was a shocked silence then some one said well what do you believe in, and I said 'people' and personal relationships. And I subjected the form to real undiluted Macmurray, about real emotion analysing one's feelings and personal relationships. Do you know I believed most of it and everyone was very impressed. Do tell K that I'm carrying the torch and preaching Macmurray among the dissolution of the acting world.

Everyone says you're working too hard, honestly Tash one can try <u>too hard</u> and that has an awfully bad effect because your work will get worse instead of better. I should ease up a bit.

Three

A WARM JUNE day in Wandsworth, south London. I have come to see Susan Downes, another old Frenshamian suggested by Shirley. I am chaining my bicycle outside her house when the door opens and a woman of about my own age comes out. 'You must be Jeremy,' she smiles. 'I'm Susan's daughter, Hannah.'

I am so startled, it is as much as I can do to shake the hand she holds out. Before I can say anything sensible, she has apologised for not being able to stay and is walking away along the pavement.

By now I am aware that someone else is standing in the open doorway — an older woman, with a mane of white hair. She suggests I bring my bike into the house, and I carry it up the steps. 'Your daughter's name,' I say, as I lean the bike against the wall. 'It isn't anything—?'

'Absolutely it is,' she says, as if nothing could be more normal, as if there are probably dozens of Hannahs named after my mother scattered around London.

My surprise must show on my face, for she says, 'I did ask Hannah if it was alright.'

'What did she say?'

'What on earth did I want to do that for? Which is what she would say, wouldn't she?'

39

I want to ask what she means by this, but she is already telling me something else — that we have met before. Susan and Hannah drifted apart after school, but they started seeing each other again in the last years of Hannah's life, and Susan remembers coming to our house in Highgate when I was two or three.

AFTER SHE HAS ushered me into the sitting room and come back with drinks, she tells me that she started at Frensham Heights several years before Hannah. Her father had died, and the headmaster then, Paul Roberts, 'who was a marvellous man', gave her and her two brothers free places.

The school was a 'very liberal establishment' and took in lots of waifs and strays. Susan was a Quaker, but there were also Jewish refugees, including a boy who had been in Belsen, though Hannah was hardly a waif or stray. She arrived when Susan was about thirteen. Hannah was a couple of years younger, but she 'had this air of sophistication about her that none of the rest of us had', and because Shirley knew her, she and Susan 'adopted' her.

I ask her to tell me more about Hannah. She was 'naturally clever', she says, and made Susan want to be clever — made her study harder. She 'could do things, everything she did she did very intensely and had to do well'. But she was also 'easily bored'. She remembers Hannah coming to stay with her in Dorset, and saying after a couple of days that she'd had enough of the countryside and wanted to go home. 'With Hannah, everything had to be exciting, heightened.'

'Is that how it was with the headmaster?'

This question seems to come out by its own volition. I hadn't meant to bring up the headmaster so soon — I wasn't sure I was going to bring him up at all — though now that I have done so, I realise he is the reason, or at least a large part of the reason, why I am here. I glance

40

at Susan nervously, but she doesn't seem to think there is anything wrong with me asking.

'I think she was fascinated by K,' she says, calling him by his first name, as Shirley had, 'but it must have been bewildering for her, too.' She leans forward conspiratorially, smoothes her white hair. 'You wrote in your article that she was fifteen, but I think she may have been fourteen when it started.'

Fourteen? Fifteen is nearly sixteen, nearly the age of consent. But fourteen is still a child. Fourteen is the age that Leah, my daughter, turned only a few days ago.

'What makes you say that?'

'I've been trying to work it out,' she says. 'My last year at Frensham, we went on a skiing holiday in Austria. Hannah had begun to confide in me by then. I remember going to her room in the hotel, and Hannah saying that K had been there, making sexual advances. I must have felt protective towards her, because one afternoon he offered to take her up the mountain, and I said I would go, too. It was already quite late when we started, and by the time we turned round it was getting dark, and Hannah got very upset. I had been skiing before, but it was her first time. She turned green, and started shaking and saying she couldn't do it.'

'What happened?'

'K talked her down, but it took a long time.'

I try to make sense of this. The bumbling headmaster of my imagination was not a skier. 'What was he like?' I say eventually.

'Tall, with bad teeth. I didn't think much of him. I found him remote and rather cold.'

'How old was he?'

'In his forties.'

If anything, I have imagined him as older, but I am still shocked to hear this. Forties is my age — the age of a father of a fourteen-year-old.

'He had this beautiful wife,' Susan says. 'We used to do sewing with her in their flat, which was at the end of the corridor from the dormitories. K's study was outside the flat. That was where Hannah used to meet him. She would walk down the corridor at night to see him.'

In my mind, I see a figure who might be Hannah, or might be Leah, walking down a long, dark corridor.

'Did she ever about talk about— ?'

'I left the school,' she says firmly, 'while it was still going on.'

'How long did it go on?'

'Two years. Maybe one. Certainly a long time.'

Two years. I had assumed a few weeks — a month or two at most.

'I don't know exactly when it ended. All I heard is that something happened — K got the wind up, perhaps he was taking too many risks, and turned cold on her. She went to his study when she hadn't been asked, and he treated her very cruelly, and she became terribly upset. I think it was why I lost touch with Hannah. I found the whole thing very disturbing.'

She stops talking, and we sit in silence.

'That was the other shocking thing about K,' she says after a while. 'Before Frensham, he taught at Bedales, and while he was there he took a party of school children to the Black Forest and lost a boy.'

'What do you mean, "lost"?'

'I don't think he was ever found. They were on a camping trip, and he got lost in the forest.'

'How do you lose a boy?'

'I don't know,' she says, her voice suddenly weary. 'I don't think I ever knew the whole story.'

From my notes, I know that we talked about other things — the Frensham production of *The Duchess of Malfi* that Sonia had mentioned, in which Susan played the duchess, and Hannah the cardinal's mistress; the smell of wisteria at the school in the spring; Susan's own subsequent career as a drama teacher — but I don't remember any of this. What I remember is my surprise that it is still day when I leave, and the pulsing in my head as I cycle away, as if someone has dropped a stone in the humid air and the ripples are spreading through me.

At home, I sit at my computer and search online for the headmaster, Frensham Heights, Bedales, lost boy, the Black Forest, but I can find nothing about any lost boy, and the only people with the headmaster's name have Facebook accounts or are running little league baseball teams.

In the morning, I cycle in to the British Library and order the few items in the catalogue on Frensham Heights and Bedales. There is a history of Frensham, but it ends with the retirement of Paul Roberts, and there are only two brief mentions of his successor as headmaster.

There isn't much about him, either, in the history of Bedales, a sort of big-sister progressive school to Frensham, other than that he taught German there from 1939 to 1949 (when presumably he moved to Frensham Heights).

In the Bedales Rolls, though, I find something. It is a who's who of old Bedalians, and while there is no entry for the headmaster (who was a teacher, not a pupil), looking under his name I find one for his wife. I read it twice — she was a prefect, captain of lacrosse, liked dressmaking and gardening — before its significance sinks in: she must have been a schoolgirl, and he one of her teachers, when they met.

ONE OF MY brother's friends, I remember, was at Bedales, and in the evening I call him. Richard wouldn't have started at the school until twenty years after the headmaster left, and all I am hoping is that he might be able to suggest someone I can speak to about him. But when I mention the headmaster's name, he laughs and says, 'I knew K.' The headmaster was a member of the old Bedalian cricket club, and as a boy Richard used to attend the summer cricket week at the school with his parents, who had both been at Bedales themselves.

Richard is not sure he ever spoke to him, but he remembers him 'turning up in a vintage Rolls, this tall, rather grand individual in a blazer, starched flannels, and a cravat, who was disapproving if he spotted grass scuffs on your flannels'.

But why, he says, am I asking about K? I don't know what to say. I hadn't expected Richard to turn the question back on me. It is one thing to talk about this with Shirley and Susan, who were Hannah's friends, who knew about what went on, but another to explain my interest to Richard, who never knew her, who has something unfashionably upright about him.

I begin to stutter about looking into Hannah's life, about the headmaster having an influence on her, but listening to my equivocations I grow angry with myself. This is my mother, after all. Why should I be embarrassed to want to know about her, ashamed of what was done to her? So I blurt it all out: about the 'affair', the long corridor, Hannah being fourteen, the lost boy.

There is a silence down the phone, and then a cough. It is the first time Richard has heard of this. He doesn't know about any incident in the Black Forest, either, and he imagines he would have heard something from his parents.

I can hear the doubts in his voice. In my family, for all I have held inside me, I have always been thought to speak too much, to be too impetuous. Simon thought this, I know, and I wouldn't be surprised if he had said it to Richard.

The people I really need to talk to are his parents, Richard says finally. The headmaster taught both of them. He was something of an influence on them — his father even went on to become a German teacher himself.

He remembers his father telling him, he says dreamily, as if holding onto a vision that my words are threatening, how the headmaster would use a cutthroat razor to shave, how his shoes were always handmade.

HE PROMISES TO TALK to his parents and get back to me in a few days, but the next morning there is a ring at the door. It is Richard, proffering a large brown envelope. 'K is the one on the right,' he says, 'with his hands in his pockets.'

When he is gone, I sit down in the kitchen and open the envelope. My heart is thumping, but the photograph I pull out could hardly be more innocent: a school cricket team in front of a thatched pavilion. 'Bedales 1st XI 1946', it says on a chalkboard propped up at their feet.

There are eleven boys in whites, and two masters on either side in umpires' coats, though it is to the one on the right that my eyes are drawn. He is tall, as Susan said, with a long nose and a thin face. His hair is smoothed back.

The photograph is grainy, his face small enough to be covered by a five-pence piece, and I bend forward to look more closely. Is that a weak chin? What about those ears — do they stick out? Is that Brylcreem on his hair?

From Richard's description, I imagined someone formal, 'grand', but when I pull back again I see it is the other teacher who stands in military fashion, with his hands behind his back, while the future headmaster is almost slouching, his hands not only in his pockets but stuffed nonchalantly there.

What does this say? Like Shirley and Susan, Richard called him by his first name. Does this mean he was friendly, easygoing? Though that isn't the impression Richard gave me — or Susan.

I look again, trying to imagine him through Hannah's eyes, though what I see is a bit-part character out of an old Ealing Studios comedy — a shopkeeper or policeman or schoolteacher.

THE ONE PERSON I have tried asking about Hannah over the years is Susie, Hannah's sister. I have always been close to Susie. She is easy to talk to, is a family therapist — her job is to get families to talk about themselves. But as with my father, the minute I mention Hannah, Susie changes, grows silent, nervous. She was seven years younger than her sister, she says, was only four when Hannah left for boarding school, doesn't remember her well, was taught, too, to forget.

But since my article came out, Susie has been sending me emails with memories of Hannah. Most are no more than glimpses. The time she and Hannah shared a double bed on a family holiday, and Hannah put a pillow between them and called it the Sword of Damocles. The time they went shopping, and Hannah left the clothes they had bought on a bus.

In one of her emails from Edinburgh, where she lives, she mentions having met a man who was in Hannah's class at school. Shirley and Susan were a year ahead of Hannah and couldn't remember her classmates, so I write to Susie asking her to explain my interest to Michael Hutchings, and a few days later I receive an email from him.

He only learned about Hannah's death a few years before, he writes, when he got back in touch with the school and, noticing that her name was missing from the class lists, 'made enquiries about her'. He wouldn't have done this for anyone else, he writes, but 'she was quite the most interesting person in my year'.

He doesn't seem to have liked her as much as he found her

interesting. His recollections are mostly about her criticising his hockey skills, or insisting on the class studying John Donne when he had suggested Milton, or how, when he directed a production of Thurber's *13 Clocks*, he didn't choose her for the role of the princess, despite her 'being the obvious choice', because if he had done so 'it would no doubt have become her show'.

His most 'striking' memory is of her 'standing up in the art room — when she was fourteen perhaps — and addressing the boys: "All you boys fancy me." Denial came there none, but I can't imagine it made her very popular among the girls.'

I read this over, trying to work out what I think about it. Something has moved on in me in the weeks since I spoke to Sonia: I am no longer disturbed by criticism of Hannah; instead, I am curious.

Michael suggests in the email that I call him if I have any questions. When I do, he is taken aback that I should think he had 'negative feelings' about Hannah — though, as the conversation continues, he admits that his feelings were 'perhaps mixed'. She was a 'very strong personality', he says.

I ask about the incident in the art room, whether anything might have prompted her to say what she did, but he says that she 'simply stood up and addressed us'. I ask if he thinks it might have had something to do with the headmaster, whether she could have been acting out what was going on with him, but his impression was that she was simply contemptuous of the boys.

He does recall another incident in which Hannah described a sexual dream while sitting at the headmaster's table at lunch, which might have had something to do with her relationship with 'Mr K', as he calls him, though he hadn't known anything about that at the time. His school days were happy, he stresses. Frensham was a happy place.

HE OFFERS TO send contact details for other members of the class. When these arrive, I send out emails, attaching my Hannah article, and within minutes I receive a reply from another classmate, Chris Harrison.

'This is a blast from the past!!!' he writes. 'I had the pleasure of knowing your mother very well at Frensham. I often wondered what became of her as we lost touch after school. Of course very sorry to hear that she died so young. I will delve into my memory banks and see what I can come up with.'

The email he sends the next morning is very different in tone, though:

> I have read, with sadness, your account of Hannah. Unfortunately, this has left me in somewhat of a dilemma. When I knew your mother, I was an innocent and gauche teenager who became unwittingly involved in the relationship between her and the headmaster, which nearly led to my expulsion from Frensham. Before I discuss this with you further, I really need to know to what ends any information I give you will be put as it certainly influenced the path my life took from then on.

He gives me his telephone number, and I call straight away, but his wife tells me he is out, playing golf. Waiting for the hours to pass, I pace the kitchen. When I stop, I notice that my legs are trembling.

When I call again, I try to sound calm, afraid that he might not be willing to talk to me, but he seems to have forgotten his reservations.

He was very fond of Hannah, he says, and for a time they were 'an item'. It was 'all very innocent, walking hand in hand to the cricket pavilion, a bit of snogging'. But then, one day, his housemaster came

48

up to him looking very grave. 'He told me I had to go up in front of K — he wouldn't say what for. I was taken to see K, and he accused me of raping Hannah. He told me he had proof, and things were going to be very difficult for me.'

The proof was a letter Hannah had apparently written to him from the sick bay, describing sexually explicit things. She had asked another girl to deliver it, and the matron had intercepted it. Chris was expelled, but after his parents — and Hannah's parents, too, he thinks — were called in, Hannah admitted she had made up the things in the letter, and his expulsion was rescinded.

I ask if he read the letter, but he never saw it, he says, and if he talked to Hannah about it he can't remember what she said. He can't say whether she had been involved with the headmaster then; he hadn't known about that at the time.

The funny thing, he says, is that the headmaster later made him head boy, but he was never comfortable again at Frensham. He was planning to be a scientist, but he lost interest in his studies and only passed two or three O levels and one A level. He talks about how his life panned out, how he went into business with his father as a commercial artist. But he keeps coming back to the incident with Hannah and the headmaster and the letter, as if he is still trying to work out what exactly it was that happened.

I KEEP COMING back to the headmaster, too. It is partly like staring at a snake; partly it feels real in a way that other stories I have heard about Hannah don't, is something I am discovering, digging up, for myself.

Though there is something else. In all the years I have lived with the knowledge that my mother killed herself, I have assumed that her death was to do with her impetuosity, something careless in her. My father said once, perhaps on that walk on Hampstead Heath, that my grandmother told him that Hannah developed passions for things and then dropped them abruptly. In my newspaper article, I offered the explanation that 'all her life she had taken things up and then thrown them aside — horses, acting, my father and, finally, life'.

What I didn't add to the list was my brother and me. What was in her mind when she left me at nursery school that afternoon? Did she turn round for a last look? How do you understand a mother who could do what she did?

But the headmaster provides an alternative narrative. That it was not that Hannah didn't love us, that she wasn't a good mother, that she didn't care, but that she was damaged by the headmaster. That she was not the seducer, but the seduced — not the instrument of her death, but the victim.

I AM A son possessed. I cycle to Paddington to meet Carole Cutner, another old Frenshamian, who shared a dormitory with Hannah and tells me how she would come back from her 'extra German coaching' with the headmaster and 'swoon onto her bed and say, "Gosh I think he's wonderful, how I love that man."'

I take the train down to Chichester to see Bill Wills, a former carpentry teacher at Frensham, now in his nineties. He remembers Hannah, remembers before I mention it that something went on her between her and the headmaster, and suggests, as Shirley did, that 'she wasn't the only one'. He remembers the headmaster coming into the common room to tell the staff that the board wanted him to retire, that he wasn't going, though he did.

I speak on the phone with Richard's mother, who doesn't know anything about Hannah, but says that the headmaster must 'have had a thing for young girls', for he 'absolutely fell' for his wife. She describes him as both 'overly friendly' and 'unknowable'. He would 'unburden himself to the sixth formers in a not entirely appropriate way, complaining that his life had been a failure'. Coming from a 'modest background', he had won a place at Cambridge University, but she felt that he had always 'really wanted to be a public-school man'.

'The thing about K,' she says, 'was that nothing ever quite came off with him. He always looked marvellous playing cricket. He had a wonderful late cut, but it was one of those strokes that only succeeded one in fifty times.'

ANOTHER EMAIL ARRIVES from Chris Harrison, with scans from a school photograph. One is of the headmaster and his wife. She is indeed beautiful, as Susan Downes said, like a 1950s film star. It is a more flattering picture of the headmaster, too: he looks handsome, distinguished, but also crueller — or am I projecting this?

Michael Hutchings also sends scans of photographs from the school magazine. One is of the woodwork room where Hannah stood up and made her pronouncement. Another is from *The Duchess of Malfi*, with Hannah as Julia, kneeling in front of the cardinal, played by a teacher.

In a blonde wig and antique dress, Hannah looks to me ethereally beautiful, as she did in her actress's headshot, but there is something in her face in this photograph, a wistfulness, a distance, that pierces my heart. She is acting, of course. *The Duchess of Malfi* is a tragedy, and I have heard how good she was in this play — but what I see, or feel that I see, awakens the father in me, makes me want to step into the photograph and rescue her.

I HAVE NEVER read or seen *The Duchess of Malfi*, but I go now to the library to get a copy. The main story is of a duchess who marries beneath her and incurs the fury of her two brothers, but it is the secondary story, of the cardinal and his mistress, that I read more closely. Julia is young, attractive, emotional. The cardinal is powerful and cold. He dresses in the robes of a churchman, but his behaviour is scarcely holy. He has a murky history, is said to have been responsible for a man's death.

The first time we see the two characters, they are arguing. Julia tells the cardinal that he wooed her with tales 'of a piteous wound i'th'heart', as Richard's mother told me the headmaster inappropriately unburdened himself to his students, and prevailed upon her beyond her strongest thoughts, as Shirley told me the headmaster wrote Hannah letters and followed her up to London. When the cardinal dismisses Julia, she makes an inappropriate play for Bosola, a servant, accusing him of putting love powder in her drink, as Hannah wrote her sexual letter to Chris Harrison.

The play wavers between seeing Julia as admirable, ahead of her time, 'a great woman of pleasure', and pitiable, confused by her sexual feelings.

It had been performed, Michael writes, in the spring of 1952, when Hannah was fifteen — in the midst, it seems likely, of her involvement with the headmaster. Was she conscious of these parallels? Did she see the play, her part, as a commentary on her own life? Is that what I see on her face?

I AM CONSCIOUS that what I am doing is not entirely rational, or healthy, but I can't stop myself. Searching again online I find a record of the headmaster's death, from cancer, in his sixties. I look him up in the 1911 census, and learn that his father was a postal sorter, his grandfather a Baptist minister. The family lived in Merton, in south London, and I peer at the satellite image of the street and think about going to see the house, though I never do.

I do cycle into the archives of the Institute of Education to read some letters he wrote to a female friend. They date from the late 1930s to the early 1940s, long before he met Hannah, and I don't expect to find much in them, but it is disturbingly thrilling to open the folder I am brought and touch the actual letters he wrote, to see his blue handwriting sloping neatly across the pages.

In only the second letter, though, sent during his first term at Bedales, he writes that he has 'fallen completely in love with two or three pupils and especially one really charming Viennese girl of about fifteen'. His correspondent is some kind of love interest, and I understand this was meant to be a joke. But a few letters on, he writes of being banned from inviting students to his rooms because of 'a rather beautiful girl' who 'does like to come and talk to me', and how the other teachers are watching his 'every move' and suspecting him of being a 'Don Juan'.

This doesn't tell me much more than I have already heard — the 'beautiful girl' was probably his future wife — but I write it all down, along with other possibly incriminating evidence. His fondness for all things German. A querulousness, an arrogance, that emerges at times (another teacher is 'an evil sham'); though I have to admit that he can also be charming, endearing. It is hard to read someone's confidences without being drawn into their point of view.

The only possible reference to the lost boy is a complaint that he has been banned from taking boys on holiday. But in a brief autobiographical note accompanying the letters is something else: 'He took a party of schoolboys ? 1935 or 1936 to Germany & tragic death of the group ? number in snowstorm in ? mountain forest.' The date explains why I could find no mention of this in the Bedales literature, why Richard had heard nothing — it was before the headmaster taught at the school. But what does 'tragic death of the group ? number' mean? Could there have been more than one lost boy?

IT IS A TANTALISING story in itself — the lost boy, lost boys even, in the forest — but it is more than that. This is the man who abused my mother, turned her into a lost girl walking down a corridor at night. I need to know what he was capable of.

Armed with this new information, I search in *The Times* online archive, and within moments I am staring at a headline from 19 April 1936: 'Caught in a Blizzard — Five London Boys Dead'.

I have to pay to read more, and I key in my credit-card details. The article that comes up is about a party of twenty-seven boys from the Strand School in Brixton, on a walking holiday in the Black Forest, led by a single teacher, twenty-eight years of age. After spending their first night at a hostel, the party set off in the morning to climb the Schauinsland mountain. There was a light sleet when they left, the paper records, but by mid-afternoon it was snowing heavily:

During the next few hours several of the boys became weaker and finally collapsed. The older ones carried their packs and helped them along until their strength also gave out. The teacher, who had been carrying the youngest boy in the party for about a mile, finally stayed behind with four of the exhausted boys and sent some stronger ones on to try to find their way down to the village. They reached the village at about 8pm. The villagers immediately formed search parties, and under great difficulties and danger to themselves twice made their way with sledges up to the exhausted boys. It was not until 11.30 pm that the last of them with their teacher was brought down to safety in the village inn, where six boys who were unconscious were given artificial respiration.

Hunched over the computer, I follow the story through the pages of the *Times*. The survivors were saved by the ringing of a church bell, which guided them to the village. The bodies were repatriated in 'black-stained coffins, made from the timber of the woods in which they died'. 'Herr Hitler' sent wreaths of 'arum lilies and fir, tied with white silk and draped in swastikas'.

An enquiry exonerated the headmaster of any blame. The unseasonal storm was 'catastrophic and beyond all calculation'. The headmaster, the inquiry concluded, showed 'courage and fortitude'. But something nags at me. I go back over the articles and read how, even after one of the boys 'showed signs of collapsing', the headmaster continued to push for the summit of the mountain.

There is something familiar about this, and I call Susan Downes and ask her again about going up the mountain with K. There were only a couple of lifts, she says, so they were taught to put skins on their skis and walk up the mountain. It was hard work, but the headmaster insisted they keep going until they reached a hut he had set as their target, even though it was already growing dangerously dark.

I go to the newspaper library in Colindale and order up other newspapers. In the *Daily Telegraph*, I read that some of the boys were already floundering 'up to their necks' in the snow when they met a group of woodcutters, who directed them on up the hill. Why had the headmaster not asked these woodcutters for help? To guide the boys back down to a village or an inn? Why had he kept going up in the storm when he could have gone down?

I go to the London Metropolitan Archives to read the report of the inquiry. From this, I learn that the headmaster had been a star pupil at the Strand School before becoming a teacher there, had been head boy, captain of football, cricket. I learn, too, that he had spent his vacations from Cambridge leading school parties on mountain excursions in the

Swiss Alps. After university, he worked in the German Alps, guiding skiing and climbing tours.

In the newspaper reports, there are contradictions and inconsistencies in the headmaster's testimony. But here, in its full length, his account is more logical. In this version of the story, the snow was not yet too deep or heavy when they met the woodcutters, and it was not so much the top of the hill for which he was heading but an inn he believed was on the other side.

I still have my suspicions — did his experience in the mountains make him overconfident? — but I am alone in them. 'I can say with a clear conscience that the master in charge of the boys behaved in a very brave and manly fashion,' one of the villagers who helped to bring the boys off the mountain testified. 'He was the last to come in from the mountain slopes where he did everything to put heart into the children and to help them out.'

The tragedy, the inquiry concludes, was caused by freak weather, not human error. The headmaster of the school, arriving in Freiburg two days later, found 'a clear sky and a hot sun — comparable to a hot June day in England'.

HERE IN LONDON, the summer is drawing on, the days shortening. I am exhausted by the past few weeks, by obsessing over Hannah and the headmaster. But I still have one more task — to go to Oxford to see Tasha Edelman.

Tasha doesn't speak on the phone, so I made the arrangements through her niece, Sonia's daughter, Becky, who also lives in Oxford.

Before going to Tasha's, I meet up with Becky. She tells me about Tasha's health. After a car accident, which caused a stroke, she had recovered and gone back to work as a psychiatrist. But subsequent strokes had diminished her.

We talk, too, about Tasha's troubles with her son and daughter from her first marriage. When the children were young, she left her husband for another man and lost custody of them, and as they grew older they refused to see her. Becky talks of Tasha leaving birthday and Christmas presents for them on the doorstep of their house, and never hearing anything. She subsequently remarried and had another daughter, but she hasn't seen her older children in years.

It is hard for me to understand: to be searching for a mother who is forever out of reach, and to hear of these children who have a mother they will not see.

BECKY DROPS ME at Tasha's house, and I follow Tasha into a back room piled with old books and magazines. The curtains are pulled shut, but the material is so thin that the sunlight shines through them and I can see the dust in the air. Tasha herself is like a ghost. The last time I saw her, more than a decade ago, she was overweight, but now her clothes hang off her. Her hair is long and grey, her eyes gazing through big round glasses. She moves and talks immensely slowly, with long pauses while she thinks or searches for the right words.

I ask her about following Hannah to Frensham.

'I would have gone anywhere to be with her,' she says.

'Why?' I ask.

She smiles. 'She was so fascinating.'

Sonia had talked when I saw her about Hannah leading Tasha into trouble, and I ask her about this.

'She always told me what to do,' Tasha says.

'Like what?'

'Split up with my boyfriend.'

'Why?'

'She decided he was bad for me.'

'Did you?'

'Yes,' she says, and a smile comes slowly again to her face. 'Then Hannah went out with him.'

'Hannah told you to split up with him, and then she went out with him?'

'Yes. Though after she finished with him, I got back together with him.'

'The thing about Hannah,' she says, after a long pause, 'was that she had to have what she wanted when she wanted it, and everyone else had to get out of the way.'

'You make her sound like a character out of *The Lord of the Flies*.'

There is another silence, and then she says, 'She was fierce, but there was also a very looking-after side of her. She looked after me.'

She talks about how Hannah was 'always smiting boys left, right, and centre'.

I ask whether serious relationships were common at the school.

'Some people went all the way,' she says.

'Was Hannah one of those?'

'I would be quite surprised if Hannah wasn't one of them.'

'Did you go all the way?'

She smiles. 'No.'

'Why not?'

'I wouldn't have known how.'

I ask how Hannah knew.

'Hannah always knew how to get into things. She was always doing, doing. She would go too far, too fast into things.'

'Is that how it was with the headmaster?'

She thinks for a while. 'I suppose it was.'

There was something 'mesmeric' about the headmaster, she says. 'When he spoke, you had to listen. You always wanted to hear what he had to say. He made you want to do well at everything.'

'Hannah was the person he cared about,' she says.

'He cared about her?'

'Yes.'

'And how did Hannah feel about him?'

'She was mad about him. For a long time, I really thought that they loved each other.'

'She loved him?'

'I think he was the love of her life before your father.'

I tell her what Susan Downes said about the headmaster being cold, how Hannah came to his study at the wrong time and he was cruel to her.

'I don't think he was cruel to Hannah,' Tasha says slowly. 'I think Hannah threw him over because she met your father.'

Can this be true? Is it her professional opinion as a psychiatrist? Or is she seeing Hannah and the headmaster through a fifteen-year-old's eyes, her understanding frozen in the past, like Hannah herself?

I ask about Hannah's suicide. She doesn't think it was depression — more not being able to see a way she could cope any more.

Cope with what? I ask.

'Not getting what she wanted.'

What did she want? I ask. But she only smiles.

I ask again about Hannah's letters. When I had spoken to Tasha on the phone several years back, she had suggested they were lost in her attic, and I offer now to go up into the attic to look for them, but she shakes her head.

It is important, I say, I have almost nothing of Hannah's, no personal writing. But she only shrugs sadly.

It has started raining outside. We sit in silence, the rain coming down. 'I do so still miss Hannah,' she says.

59

Autumn 1953

Dear Tash, So far this weekend has been a real 'experience'. Jill and I arrived in Cambridge at about eleven am on Saturday and I waited for Sonia who was of course half an hour late. The town was in an uproar. It was poppy day and everyone was out collecting in fancy dress. Lorries with St Trinian girls, Everest snowmen, in fact everything under the sun.

Sonia has quite a nice room but she hasnt alas (like me) got any fatter, though she swears she eats all day long, as do everyone else! We had lunch in hall which was lousy, and then struggled through the crowds again to see Sonia in a play. On the way I first met Trevor, who was standing on a wall shouting in a very Trevorish fashion, and then I met Jeremy who has invited me to tea with him today. Sonia only had one line — but she was excellent and showed great signs of talent. Then alas we had an enormous tea, and after went to a revue done by St Johns — it was lousy. Then we went with Michael P to a party. He seems very keen on Sonia! At first I felt very lost, but then I got talking to a rather good looking boy called — K!! who must be about twenty three he is in his third year, writes for Varsity, he invited me to lunch today. I also met a boy I had seen at Shirley's very intelligent and rather ugly called David. He invited me for a drink at 12 today.

I am now at home having left PARADA at 1.30 pm because I was too tired to stay any longer. I went for the drink at David's & had an enormous gin and French which made me quite dizzy. Then he and K took me to an enormous lunch at an Indian Restaurant during which K said he would be in London on Tuesday & would ring me in the evening and probably take me to Casa Pepe's and then to a Jazz Club, which sounds very interesting but I have my doubts as to whether he'll ring me. He has <u>lovely</u> eyes.

60

I looked all round Cambridge. Its very lovely, there is an immense atmosphere of repose in the vast courtyards and along the river banks with the weeping willows. But I'd <u>hate</u> to be there! Newnham is vile it looks like a gas works and all the men utterly despise Newnham and Girton. I had tea and supper with Jeremy who for the first time I feel quite natural with. He is very nice, but thoroughly debauched, and, so he says repressed! He tried to kiss me, but I wouldn't have it! Apart from the fact that I am dead tired and horribly fat life is quite pleasant.

Four

ONE LATE SUMMER WEEKEND, Susie comes down from Edinburgh with a suitcase of my grandparents' papers. From my memories of sorting though their house, I don't expect there to be a treasure trove of Hannah material here, but I am still disappointed at how little there seems to be: a folder of early poems and drawings, reports from her primary school, some photographs.

Of the usual teenage paraphernalia of diaries, letters, schoolbooks, photographs like those Shirley showed me, there is no sign. Though Hannah spent five years at boarding school, there are none of the letters she must have written to her parents. Unless Hannah got rid of her teenage things when she left home, they must have been discarded either by my grandparents or my father. Suicide not only ends a life, it changes how that life is remembered. The happy, hopeful times are refracted through the end, invalidated by the act of the death.

Most of the papers are my grandfather's unpublished typescripts. He published half a dozen books, as well as hundreds of articles and essays, but these are various attempts at a memoir. To my grandfather, though, memoir meant recollections of his times, the people he met, rather than his own personal life, and there again seems to be disappointingly little about Hannah.

It is a relief, though, after the turbulence of the past weeks, to hear my grandfather's familiar wry voice in my head. He was the wisest man, at least in the ways of the broader world, I have known, and I loved talking to him, listening to him. And as I read, I find, tucked away in his portraits of interesting people and times, occasional mentions of his family. From these fragments, and others in his published books, along with clues Susie continues to send, and conversations with her, I begin to piece together Hannah's early life.

SHE WAS BORN, I know, in Palestine, but I learn now how my grandparents had come to be there. They had met and married in London, where my grandfather had lived since his wandering Zionist parents had brought him there at the age of thirteen, and my grandmother had come from the small town in South Africa where she had grown up to 'go to the theatre and see art galleries'. My grandfather was working as a floorwalker, or trainee manager, at Marks and Spencer, and writing a novel. When his novel was published without much notice, he threw in his job and they sailed to South Africa to visit my grandmother's family, and it was on the way back that they stopped in Palestine.

They had meant to stay only a few weeks, to see my grandmother's brother and sister, and my grandfather's father, who had settled there. But my grandfather was still working out what to do with his life, and through his father's Zionist connections he got a job at the Jewish Federation of Labour. My grandmother also found work at a school run by a disciple of Freud in Tel Aviv, and it was in this modern city rising out of the sands, on 19 August 1936, that Hannah was born.

Two early influences on Hannah's life emerge from my grandfather's writings. One is a memory of standing at the glass looking at his newborn daughter, and his sister-in-law beside him saying, '*Das Kind ist klug*' — that child is clever. It was something Hannah had to live up to all her life: that she was clever, precocious, that things were expected of her.

More immediate was the world into which she was born. My grandfather was reading newspaper reports from the Spanish Civil War when a nurse came to tell him that he had a daughter: 'I was only too well aware that in Hannah I had acquired a new and special responsibility and there was world war looming ahead.' Hannah was always known as Hannah, but the name on her birth certificate was Ann — the English, non-Jewish, version of the name.

There is nothing more in my grandfather's writings about Hannah's first year and a half, but among the material Susie brought is a small photograph album that gives a sense of her early life in Tel Aviv. Here are my grandparents holding Hannah proudly in a flat furnished with the sparse austerity of settler life. Here is her nanny pushing her in a wicker pram along dirt roads past low stone apartment buildings. And here she is, a year or so later, riding a tricycle, toddling into the sea, with the broad smile I know from later photographs, looking at different times remarkably like both my daughters.

An 'enchanting sprite', my grandfather wrote, in his one written recollection of her in Palestine:

Small, slender, agile, she was enormously precocious. At eighteen months, when we were passing a kindergarten, Hannah ran inside, insisted on joining in the game and there she remained and held her own. Now she was twenty months, she was running in an imagined game through our apartment, she spoke in clear sentences and then started out on what she unfortunately already knew was her parlour trick: reciting from her Babar books, which she knew by heart, and turning the pages at the right word, as if reading.

By now, my grandfather had given up his job to write a book about the prospects of Palestine. He had grown up in a Zionist household, and he writes of falling 'under the passions of that insecure little land'. Returning from a tour of kibbutzim, with their utopian dreams, he 'felt suddenly and uneasily aware of the barrenness, the hollowness, of Western middle-class life'. But it is interesting that his Zionism didn't blind him to the aspirations of the Palestinian Arabs, and the prescient thesis of his book, with its equally prescient title, *No Ease in Zion*, was to advocate a combined Jewish–Arab state.

In his later years, he followed Israel's progress closely, still arguing for more pro-Arab policies, increasingly saddened by how those utopian dreams had turned out, but it is only now that I realise how close he and my grandmother came to throwing in their lot with Zionism and staying in Palestine. How differently Hannah's life would have turned out, though I wouldn't be here to write about it. But as it was, more powerful than my grandfather's attraction to Palestine was his desire to be a writer. When the news broke that Hitler had annexed Austria in March 1938, the 'action for a writer', he decided, was in Europe, and he flew back to London, my grandmother and Hannah following more slowly by sea.

IN LONDON, my grandparents rented a little house in the Vale of Health, on the edge of Hampstead Heath. Hannah, now nearly two, 'briefly produced a sleep disturbance and crying fits'. Removed from her home and her nanny, this was hardly surprising, but my grandmother's work in Tel Aviv had turned her into a confirmed Freudian, and hearing that the Freuds themselves were living only a short walk away, she wrote to Anna Freud for help.

Anna Freud 'wrote back with exquisite politeness that she could not yet take cases', but suggested another refugee psychoanalyst,

Marianne Kris, who agreed to see Hannah. My grandfather recalled with a mixture of amusement and fascination how 'the eminent Dr Kris at once gained Hannah's attention, gave her a Daddy doll, a Mummy doll, a Hannah doll and a nanny doll, and asked her to play a game'. Separation anxiety was duly diagnosed, and after being prescribed some extra cosseting, Hannah was soon running about with her 'usual zest'.

My grandmother enrolled her at a nursery school in Highgate, and in the mornings, waiting for the school bus to pick her up, her excitement 'was so great she could not contain herself, hopping madly from leg to leg'. She soon acquired the 'precise, high pitched enunciation of English upper-middle class children'.

This new life was not to last long, though. To my surprise, I learn that in the summer of 1939, whether with the intention of escaping the looming war or of taking Hannah to see her parents before war made this impossible, my grandmother and Hannah sailed for South Africa. Equally surprising, my grandfather set off on travels around Europe, taking in, among other places, Berlin, where he wandered 'among the "No Jews Desired" notices like a spook'. He had spent his early years in Strasbourg and Zurich, but he was born in Cologne, and he wrote how grateful he was for his British passport.

Whatever her intentions in travelling to South Africa, my grandmother must have decided to outrun the war back to Europe, for by the winter of 1939 the family was together again in a guest house on the Ridge in Hastings. Perhaps they had chosen that spot so my grandfather could gaze across the sea to France, 'the waters silvery in the moonlight along the blacked coast'. In September 1939, he had 'stood for a day in a senseless queue of volunteers outside the War Office'; but in his efforts to sign up, his German birth counted against him, and instead he began writing a book about racial equality, influenced by what he had seen both in Germany and South Africa, to which he had taken a dislike from the moment his ship 'arrived in Cape Town and I saw the black African porters in their cast-offs standing on the dock below like accusing dark shadows'.

In the mornings, he or my grandmother took Hannah on the trolley bus to her new school. When it snowed, she 'played boisterously in the deep snow with two friendly Alsatian dogs'. In May, the Germans attacked the Maginot Line, and three weeks later the family watched the flotilla of boats sail for Dunkirk.

By summer they had moved again — into a farmhouse near Twyford, in Berkshire, with my grandfather's publisher, Fred Warburg, and his wife. Warburg introduced my grandfather to George Orwell, who was a frequent visitor, and the three of them came up with the idea of the Searchlight series of books on war aims — my grandfather's book on race, *The Malady and the Vision*, would be one; Orwell's *The Lion and the Unicorn*, another.

Hannah, now nearly four, and the only child in the house, was 'the little queen of the place'. My grandfather wrote of 'Fred Warburg, that haughty publisher, lying on his back in the grass and holding her high in the air' and 'Orwell, stretched out on the grass, reading Hauff's fairy tales to her'.

She was already on her fourth educational establishment, a few miles away in Sonning, to which she travelled on her own by Green Line coach. Returning one afternoon, my grandfather recalled, 'she asked for the stop too late, and the coach overshot the stop where I was waiting by three-quarters of a mile. Hurrying in that direction, I came upon the tiny figure running towards me along the Great West Road with a tear-stained face, nearer, nearer, and into my arms.'

The arrangement at Scarlett's Farm was not to last either, though, and by the following summer my grandparents and Hannah had moved again, this time more permanently, to the cottage outside Amersham.

My grandfather was in England for another couple of years, but he was working for the BBC, and later the Foreign Office, in London, and there is no mention of life in Amersham in any of his writings from that period. In 1943, he was finally taken into the army as a psychological warfare officer and he sailed for Algiers. His years in the army were good times for him, and his memoirs record his travels through north Africa and Italy, where he interrogated prisoners at Monte Cassino. But from the story of Hannah's life his voice now fades, at least for a few years.

ON A COLD late autumn day, I drive out to Amersham. Susie has told me that the cottage was on London Road and was called Evescot, but the name must have been changed, for the only reference I can find online to Evescot, London Road, is a notice from 1942 of my grandfather's anglicising of the spelling of his surname from the original Feiwel to Fyvel, in his efforts to get into the army.

Susie told me it was one of a row of a dozen-or-so cottages, and with her directions I find the cottages without too much difficulty. I had always understood that Hannah lived on the edge of town, but it is a mile outside Amersham here, cars speeding past, and fields climbing hills on both sides of the road.

Susie was four when they moved away, and the only clues she could give me is that Evescot was towards the southern end of the row; that 'Clarkie', or Mrs Clark, the housekeeper Hannah locked in the chicken shed, lived next door; and that there was a cherry tree outside the front door.

I walk along the row, examining the cottages. A couple have cherry trees out front, and I pick one of these and ring the bell on the door behind it. A middle-aged man eventually comes to the door. He has been here for twenty years, he says, but none of the cottages was ever called Evescot, as far as he knows, and he doesn't remember any Clarks living here. No one else has been here as long as he has. I explain my interest, peer past him hopefully. This could be the cottage where my mother lived. But he does not take the hint, does not invite me in.

I drive up to the local library, but there is no information there. I call Sonia, but she can't help either. Susie says she would recognise the cottage if she saw it, and suggests we drive out together next time she is in London, though she is not due down for a few weeks and I am impatient. It is hard to explain why it is so important to me, but it is: this is the cottage where Hannah grew up, where she lived in the stories that until recently were all I knew of her childhood.

I think about the Clarks. Susie says they stayed on at London Road after the Fyvels left, and though she doesn't know where they went, it is not unlikely that they remained in the area. Clarkie would surely be dead by now, but what about her son, Roger, Hannah's friend in my grandmother's stories?

Clark is a common name, and I am not sure it wasn't Clarke or even Clerk, but searching online I discover a Roger Clark from Amersham, of about the right age, who belongs to a vintage-car club, and through this I get his phone number.

When I call, Roger seems almost as delighted to hear from me as I am to have found him. Evescot was the third cottage from the left, he says. The Clarks's was the end cottage. They lived there until 1961. Hannah came with my grandmother to visit when he was about fourteen or fifteen, he remembers, but he stayed in his room and refused to come downstairs.

HIS WIFE IS about to have an operation, but he would be happy to see me after that. Less impatient now that I have found him, I suggest a day when Susie will be in London, and a couple of weeks later, Susie and I drive out to Amersham.

On the way, Susie reminds me of my grandmother's stories, some of which I have forgotten. The incident with the chicken shed was apparently part of a broader campaign Hannah waged against Clarkie. On another occasion, she helped Roger escape when Clarkie locked him in his room by instructing him to tie sheets together and climb out of his window. She also orchestrated the local children to hide in the brambles when Clarkie went blackberrying and to jump out at her. These stories carry me so readily back to the images in my childhood mind that I am almost surprised when we knock on Roger's door and it is answered by a smiling grey-haired man and not the boy of my imagination.

In his sitting room, Roger shows us a picture of himself as exactly the gap-toothed boy I pictured. Though when we tell him about my grandmother's stories, he corrects us. His mother may have helped my grandmother out with eggs — it was her chicken shed — but she wasn't anyone's housekeeper. Nor was she ever cruel to him.

He and Hannah, he tells us, were part of a gang of children living in the cottages who went around stealing apples and walnuts from people's gardens, picking mushrooms, hunting squirrels with homemade catapults. The men were mostly gone to war, and the fields and woods and roads were empty. In those days, you could wait for an hour for a car to come along London Road.

There was a rubbish dump a little further along, and they would search through it for anything they might be able to use — old toys, bicycle parts. They found a bathtub once, and dragged it down to the river, and plugged up the hole and used it as a boat. At night they would sit on the dump, smoking cigarettes.

All this is new to me — Hannah the tomboy, as Roger describes

71

her, running wild with her countryside gang. Though I wonder how much these are Roger's stories, how much Hannah was actually present in them, whether she wouldn't often have been at Chesham Bois or gymkhanas with Sonia and Tasha.

He had seen Hannah coming up the drive, Roger says, the time she and my grandmother came to visit when he was fourteen or fifteen, and had shouted down to his mother to say he wasn't there. Why? I ask. 'Because she looked so beautiful and sophisticated' and he was 'a teenage boy with acne'. He stayed in his room until they left. That glimpse out of the window was the last time he saw her.

AFTERWARDS SUSIE and I stop at the cottages. We know which one was Evescot now, but it refuses to look any different from the others. She asks if I want to ring the bell, and I shake my head. I don't need to see inside any more; it is enough to have met Roger, heard his memories.

On the way home, Susie tells me more about those times. I knew my grandmother as she was in her older years, fastidious about dirt on her carpets in her Primrose Hill house, at war with the cats that defecated in her garden, but Susie says she enjoyed her years in the country. She didn't have a car, but she could cycle or take the bus to get around. Her cousin, Lila, often stayed with her and 'taught her to drink': they would go to the pub in the evening and 'drink gin, brandy, rum, whatever they could get'. Together, Susie says, the two women 'discovered that life could be pleasant without men'.

Hannah, too, seems to have thrived in a female household. When Lila's dog had to be taken to the vet to be put down, the three of them took her together, and Hannah had the idea of singing hymns to cheer them all up, and soon the whole of the upper deck of the Green Line bus was singing along.

Among my grandparents' papers are a handful of letters my grandmother sent to my grandfather during the war. In one, dated October 1943, she wrote of a visit from an army friend. Hannah, then seven, was 'very sweet and anxious to hear all about her Daddy. She came down in her night-gown and a lovely red velvet cloak. She looked very charming and behaved in a delightful way.'

Most of the references to Hannah are about her achievements: reading *Oliver Twist* at seven, writing four poems in an evening — though one mention, while complimentary, hints at a more challenging girl. She is 'on top of her form. She is so helpful and so very easy. I can't remember when I last had a scene.'

The poems in the folder Susie brought are all from this period. They include several that were published in a children's periodical and one broadcast on the BBC, presumably the competition of my grandmother's story. They are precocious for a seven- or eight-year-old. 'Like water from the ocean great,' reads one, 'Women weep about the gate. /The canary up on the wall /Has watched us sobbing in the hall.' But they are all imitative like this, don't say much about her other than that she was clever, good at fulfilling adult expectations.

Her precocity did lead to her being pushed ahead a year in school. In her first school report from St Mary's School in Gerrards Cross, she was just five while the average age of the class was six and a half. 'Hannah has settled in and made good progress this term,' her early reports read. 'Hannah has a very good memory, quite a wide vocabulary.' But comments about her intelligence and abilities were soon being tempered by concerns about her attitude. 'Hannah's enthusiasm is delightful but she needs to learn not to be assertive and to realise that other people are equally important.' 'Hannah is inclined to demand too much attention.' 'She is still too noisy, and must learn both to speak and to move more quietly.'

These reports seem to me more revealing of Hannah's personality than her poems, if not always perhaps in the way that the teachers intended. I don't doubt that she was assertive, boisterous, noisy, but I wonder if there would have been so much concern about these characteristics if she had been a boy.

Among the papers Susie brought are also some photographs from the Amersham days. One is a school photograph in which Hannah stands at the end of a row, half the size of the other children, her hair in pigtails, a proud smile on her face.

Several are of Hannah riding in a pair of oversized jodhpurs. In one, she is galloping, bent forward over the horse's mane, a fierce expression on her face. In another, she is standing on the saddle of the horse.

Most moving to me are a couple of contact sheets taken several years apart, presumably at a portrait studio. Each consists of forty-eight shots, and looking from one shot to the next is almost like watching a clip of film.

In the first, she is five or six, wearing a coat with a hood. She is clearly being asked to smile, but she keeps forgetting and starts looking around, and then is told to smile again and does so, more and less genuinely.

In the second, she is perhaps nine or ten. She is wearing a polka-dot blouse and a little white bow in her hair. She is a bit more toothy and gawky, more self-conscious. In some of the shots she grins broadly, but in others she purses her mouth as an older girl might do, or is caught looking sideways at the camera, and it seems to me that I see on her face a sense of expectation, a readiness, impatience, for the adventure of life to come.

Winter 1953

Dear Tash, I have begun to learn ballet which is foul!! I am so like an elephant its hard to believe! I am leading a very quiet life I dont want to go out much as I have a lot of work to do — lying on the ground breathing in and out.

I had a sweet letter from K — rather pathetic really — he is sweet.

I have just done a scene of The Young Elizabeth as Mary. Its funny I felt the part today which I havent done for ages. The trouble is Mary was all skin and bones, which I am most definitely not! But its very good for me because I have to hold myself very straight and cant do any of my wriggling tricks. Did you know that I wriggled?

Dear Tash, I feel I am becoming rather a hermit — for example I had two different invitations to go to two different parties yesterday evening, and didn't go to either, instead I went to bed early and slept like a log. Actually one reason was that the night before was the PARADA dance, which was quite good fun. Afterwards we went off to London Airport and sat in the Restaurant eating spagetti and melon (separately) and drinking black coffee until about 5 a.m. with the result that yesterday I felt absolutely bloody.

My voice is my main bugbear in acting but it is only really a reflection of something inside me. If acting doesnt do anything else it does teach you about yourself. Its amazing Tash, I know so much more about myself now. One of the teachers said to me — deep inside you Hannah, you have a kind sincere nature and you have a great deal to give, but on top of that there is a protective layer of hardness, selfishness and pride, and that is holding back what lies underneath.

76

I have come to a conclusion about myself. You see at Frensham I was never really allowed to be myself — everyone thought I was hard, tough etc etc and so I had to be. But at PARADA I started off by being much more gentle, and I get on better with more people than I ever did before. You know that I am not really a bit tough.

Five

AT THE END of the war, my grandfather came home to meet Susie for the first time and to find Hannah 'grown into a slim athlete in jodhpurs'. I had always assumed that the family had moved straight into London, but in fact they stayed in the cottage, and after that another nearby house, for a further six years.

With London easily accessible on the Metropolitan line, my grandfather soon had a job as literary editor of *Tribune*, and there is no further mention in his writings of his home life. My main source of information about Hannah's years in Buckinghamshire after the war are the cups and rosettes she won at pony club meetings, which tell of weekends at places like Hyde Heath and Cherry Dell, or High Wycombe and Beaconsfield, and even as far away as the East Sussex Riding Club in Crowhurst, on the other side of London.

Among my grandparents' papers is a programme from one of these meetings. For younger children there was 'bending' — a kind of slalom on horseback — and simple dressage and 'saddling up', but as the girls got older the jumping grew more serious. My grandmother told of Hannah competing against Olympic riders, and my grandfather wrote of Hannah and Alan Oliver, who rode for England, if not at the Olympics, 'winning everything'. Photographs also show an older Hannah, grown into her jodhpurs, riding over some serious jumps.

One of the rosettes was for winning the Juvenile Open Jumping Competition at the British Show Jumping Association. Another, when Hannah was eleven, was for 'Best child rider under 21'. There is also a grand 'Turf and Travel Cup', with a sterling silver hallmark. Most of the prizes, though, are from local meetings, and as many are for second or third as first place, suggesting that there were other riders as good or better than she was — that though she must have been a talented rider, her abilities as a horsewoman seem to have grown after her death.

The cups and rosettes suggest she peaked in the summer of 1948, when she turned twelve, the autumn before she started at Frensham Heights. She didn't throw over riding as abruptly as my grandmother told my father; she continued to win prizes for the next couple of summers, though less each season, and by the time she turned fourteen her interests had moved on.

THERE WERE PLENTY of good day schools within reach of Amersham; Sonia was already at nearby Berkhamsted. But Susie remembers my grandparents telling her how eager Hannah was to go away to boarding school, and sensing that they had not been unhappy to see her leave.

Frensham Heights, with its emphasis on self-expression and the arts, including drama, was certainly a more natural home for Hannah than St Mary's in Gerrards Cross. The one report from Frensham that has survived among my grandparents' papers, from her first term, shows an immediately more sympathetic appreciation of her character: 'Alert and critical, Hannah very soon learnt the way of things. She has made friends and was generally the first to make contact. We are pleased with the way she has settled down to living in a dormitory. In managing her own routine affairs she is quick and capable.'

I have continued to be passed from one old Frenshamian to another, and most use similar words to describe Hannah: 'exuberant',

80

'fascinating', 'a character', 'always smiling, always happy', 'dynamic but also highly emotional'. 'Dramatic was the word we used,' Carole Cutner told me.

Time and age make more specific memories harder to elicit. Tasha remembered Hannah deciding that the girls were all too fat, and getting a group of them to meet in the locker rooms in the morning to exercise while she chanted Shakespeare at them: 'Oh that this too too solid flesh would melt.'

Bill Wills, the carpentry teacher, recalled some girls who had signed up for carpentry to 'get out of sewing' pushing the clock hand forward in his workshop so they could leave early. 'I think Hannah was one of them,' he said, with a wink.

She was 'several teachers' pet', according to Carole Cutner, though another old Frenshamian remembered her getting into trouble with a teacher for referring to local people as 'yokels'; and Susan Downes remembered a disagreement with another teacher that ended with Hannah 'turning a whitish green and shaking', as she had on the ski slopes with the headmaster.

One or two former classmates are more critical. Stephen Frank, who Susan perhaps meant by the boy who had been in Belsen, though it was actually Teresienstadt, talks of Hannah's need to 'rule the roost'. And I have an email exchange with a woman Susie remembers as Hannah's friend who eventually writes to say she would rather not speak about Hannah.

More surprising to me is that Hannah was an athlete. I know about her riding and that she was a good water skier and skier. But it is still unexpected to hear that she was 'good at the long jump, the high jump, sprinting, and fast on the wing at hockey'. There is something particularly poignant in the thought of a teenage Hannah running eagerly down the wing in her hockey kit.

PERHAPS WHAT I find moving is the contrast between the innocence of that image and the one of her walking down the corridor at night to the headmaster's study. Other than Shirley, Susan, and Tasha, Hannah's other contemporaries don't seem to have known about Hannah and the headmaster at the time, though they heard about it later. But all noticed her interest in boys, and boys' interest in her.

I know about Chris Harrison, and have been told about another Frensham boyfriend. Then there was the 'Robert something foreign' Shirley mentioned, who I learn was Robert Landori Hoffman, a name it is easy to track down to Canada, where he lives. He remembers Hannah 'as a slight, pretty black-haired girl', he writes back when I email him. 'Of course we were all so very young then.' He gives me his number in Montreal, and I call him. He was a couple of years older than Hannah, but they had a 'pash' for each other. 'Everyone was always having pashes,' he says. 'An innocent word but they were not always so innocent, there was a lot of fumbling in the bushes.'

I can't bring myself to ask Robert about his fumblings with my mother, but I do start keeping a list of her inamoratos. There was the boy on the Sweden trip, and Susie also mentions that at Simon's funeral an old friend of my father's, Hamish MacGibbon, told her that Hannah had been his first love.

I call Hamish, and go round to see him. He was sixteen when he met Hannah, he says. His parents and my grandparents were friends, and his mother, who was always trying to fix him up, kept nagging him about this attractive girl. He was reluctant at first, but once he met Hannah he was 'crazy about her'. He took her sailing on the Thames and to watch the fireworks at the Festival of Britain.

He remembers riding home with her in a taxi one evening and telling the driver to keep driving round the outer circle in Regents Park so he could kiss her. She had this 'lovely sense of humour and

82

a combination of good looks and a sharp mind'. He is in his eighth decade now, on his second wife, but his eyes grow misty at the memory. 'I think I was probably in love with her,' he says.

Hannah was fifteen at the time, he thinks, but when I get home I look up the date of the Festival of Britain and see that she was still fourteen — young, back then, to be kissing in the back of taxis.

I ALSO GO to see Jill Steinberg, another person I always thought was my father's friend, but who, Sonia told me, knew Hannah from Amersham days. Jill says that for a time in their teens, when they were about fourteen, she and Hannah were close in the way girls can be. She was flattered by Hannah's attentions, she says, but was also wary. 'When Hannah focused on you it was very intense, but you were aware that at any time the focus might move on somewhere else.'

They were the same age, but Hannah was more mature, more 'knowing'. Jill remembers them writing, 'or really Hannah writing', to *Woman's Own* magazine for information about birth control. Hannah insisted that they give Jill's address — Jill's parents were less likely to notice a letter arriving for her than my grandparents. The letter duly came, and Jill remembers reading the material with Hannah on a bus going down Regent Street. To Jill, birth control, the whole idea of sex, was something to giggle over, but 'looking back now' she thinks that Hannah had really wanted to know about it.

TYPING UP MY notes from these conversations, I imagine my own teenage daughters looking over my shoulder and telling me to leave the poor girl alone, to get myself a life. I am learning more about my mother's adolescent romances than most sons would know, or would want to know. This obsession with her love life is partly, I realise, about the headmaster again. How do her 'pashes' with boys relate to what she was doing with him? But it is more than that. She killed herself, after all, over a man, over a failed love affair — or so the story goes.

I am conscious that everything I am hearing is looked at through the prism of time, fading memories. So I am excited when Shirley writes to say that she has found her teenage diaries and is typing up any references to Hannah, which she sends a few days later.

The entries start in January 1949, six months after Hannah started at Frensham. They are still clearly little girls. They go to a 'super smashing circus', and afterwards Hannah stays the night at Shirley's.

Friendships between girls dominate, and several entries are about a girl I realise is the woman who didn't want to speak about Hannah. She and Hannah have 'broken up', Shirley writes. The girl and another are 'being vile to Han', who is 'coming round with us as she's no one to go around with'. Shirley doesn't say what happened, and I can't imagine it was too serious, though serious enough, it seems, for the woman not to want to speak about Hannah sixty years later.

By autumn of the next year — the period Hannah gave up riding — the focus had turned to boys. Hannah, now fourteen, has quarreled 'like hell' with Chris, and Shirley has had to intervene, or 'in-between', as she calls it. 'They do get so intense about it,' she writes. 'During senior supper they are still at it.'

Another year on, and Hannah is with Robert Landori-Hoffman. She 'really cannot stop talking about Robert', and gets 'frightfully jealous' if anyone else 'as much as glances in his direction'. Speaking in the bathroom late one night, Hannah tells Shirley how she and Robert 'had been making hay apparently in the senior sitting room and K caught them and was fairly icy. Hanny was worried stiff, said that K hated her etc, which is of course balderdash.'

A few weeks later, Shirley writes of Hannah slapping Robert. 'He was livid. Silly idiots.' Soon after, they have broken up. At first, Hannah is 'very cut up about it' and 'frantic and furious' when she sees Robert with another girl. But a few months later, she comes back from the boating holiday in Sweden 'brown and attractive' and 'apparently madly in love'.

Shirley had left Frensham by now, and there is only one more entry, from the skiing holiday in Austria that Christmas, which Shirley, like Susan, went on despite no longer being at the school. Perhaps Hannah's explicit letter to Chris Harrison was not caused by the headmaster but an eye-opener to him, his catching Hannah 'making hay' with Robert, too, for he seems now to have taken their place: 'Gosh but she is getting attractive, far more than I am and when I am with her I cannot control a slight feeling of jealousy. As for Hannah and K, on the journey, whether by coincidence or planning, Hannah was constantly by him and during the night literally slept in his arms, confiding to me afterwards he kissed her four times on the lips in brotherly fashion. I was shocked.'

I HAVE BEEN in contact with a woman named Rosellen in the Frensham Heights alumni office about visiting the school, and one morning I take the train down with Carole Cutner. When we arrive, Rosellen and Carole show me round the main house, which was originally built for the Charrington brewing family. We walk through the old ballroom, where children are having a dance lesson. 'Where we had our dances every Saturday night,' Carole says, 'the girls lined down one wall, the boys down the other.' On the other side is the old orangery, apparently the last to be built in Europe. The house stands on the lip of a hill, and there are views across the valley to the fields and tree-lined hills on the other side.

When Rosellen goes back to work, Carole takes me up the grand central staircase to the dormitories where she and Hannah lived, though they are about to be refurbished and are empty except for a few dusty beds and desks.

We find the room Carole shared with Hannah. It is smaller than I expected, with space for only three or four beds. We go, too, into the headmaster's study, and I look around, trying to see ghosts, though it is only another dusty room. When we come back out, I realise we are standing in the corridor Hannah walked along to see the headmaster, though it is shorter, less gothic, than I imagined. On one of the bare walls, a corner peeling away, is a poster for Childline.

LATER WE GO downstairs to read the material Rosellen has dug up from the late 1940s and early 1950s. I had hoped there might be copies of Hannah's reports, but Rosellen explains that most of the old records are in unsorted boxes in the cellars. What is here are photographs and old school magazines.

Leafing through the magazines, I find reviews of school plays Hannah was in. Her first part, when she was thirteen, was as a maid in *Tobias and the Angel*, by James Brodie, but a year later she had claimed her first lead, as Cleopatra in Shaw's *Caesar and Cleopatra*. Hannah 'made Cleopatra precocious without being aggressive and kittenish without affectation', the review says. Photographs show her in a long black wig, sleek and womanly. 'At the time of the play,' the review says, 'Cleopatra is sixteen years old and Caesar fifty-two.'

I also find some articles Hannah wrote, about a swimming event, her French exchange trip ('I saw all the things that one should see and a few that one should not'), and a day spent collecting money for charity — or not collecting money, as she and Tasha had somehow picked a road that didn't exist.

They meet a man pushing a cart of logs who 'burst forth in a torrent of words to the effect that he had lived here for sixty years and never in his life had he heard of Ellerslie Lane'. He goes off 'muttering in sepulchral tones' and they try a different road, but other Frensham Heights students have already been here. After meeting a dog that takes 'an instantaneous aversion to us', they return to school and hear from a boy about 'a tussle with a lady who had tried desperately to persuade him to take a feather bed instead of money'.

IN THE MAGAZINES are also the headmaster's annual speech day addresses, with their emphasis on the wellbeing of the students. On the train back, I ask Carole what she thinks went on during Hannah's 'extra German coaching', but all she thought at the time, she says, was that Hannah had a crush on him.

I have heard from Shirley and Bill Wills, the carpentry teacher, that Hannah wasn't the 'only one', and Tasha even named a girl she said had been Hannah's 'successor' in the headmaster's affections. I haven't done anything about this; but when I ask Carole now, she says she is still in touch with this woman and offers to contact her, and a few days later the woman sends me an email.

'You must remember that Hannah was not a very special friend of mine and it is now all more than fifty years ago,' she writes. 'I would however hope to be able to help a little in your understanding of her suicide.' She gives me her phone number, and suggests a time to call. It is a few hours away, and as the time passes I become increasingly more nervous, convinced I am about to discover the secrets of the headmaster's study.

But when we speak it turns out there has been a misunderstanding. Nothing inappropriate took place between her and the headmaster, she insists. She only has favourable things to say about him.

What she meant about suicide was that she has had some professional experience of the subject. The problem was the coal gas used in homes in those days, with its high content of carbon monoxide in its natural state, which made it easier for people to kill themselves. When the switch was made to natural gas, the suicide rate dropped by a third.

Winter – Spring 1954

Dear Tash, I miss you and feel very lonely especially at RADA. I've ceased to be bewildered by all the long corridors and many staircases but the atmosphere is still the same — very impersonal — so unlike Frensham. The woman who is producing our play is very efficient but totally uninspiring. The diction woman is a complete wet rag, and the other staff are better but none of them really make any personal contact with us, I mean outside what they are teaching. I'm afraid I'm too used to K. I still miss him like hell, but I'm jolly well going to get over that.

Val absolutely adores Richard, & I spent an evening in which she kept telling me how much she wanted to kiss him, but knew she mustnt because that was cheapening herself — she thought there was nothing between kissing and sleeping with someone. I assured her that there was masses of things in between! I do think a girl of 18 should know a bit more than that.

My dear Tash, I am hopeless as Lion — I just can't play comedy. Its my voice thats my main trouble. I have a slight South African accent, and I drop the ends of my phrases my vowels are bad. Oh dear at this rate I shall never make an actress.

I wrote to K about a week ago and had no answer as yet — I do miss him terribly some times. I feel very bitter, because I know he just doesnt care a whit anymore — but it isn't fair to him for me to be bitter — Oh I don't understand if I think about it I feel hellish so try not to think about it.

I had a very long & miserable letter from Mike! I am absolutely determined to go to Israel in the summer.

Dear Tash, I had a most alarming experience last Friday, you may or may not know that there was an Old Frenshamian meeting at David's and Shirley persuaded me to go. Well I hadn't been there five minutes when in walked K! Shirley said I went quite white and looked as if I was going to faint — I felt as if I was going to I assure you. He has never been to a meeting before and it isn't conceit if I say that he really only came to see me. Well it took me about an hour to be able to speak to him and then when I did I felt as if I was going to dissolve! Can you imagine he was standing drinking Coca Cola! Most incongruous! We chatted a bit, and then Shirley and I decided to go, and he said he was going too! He gave us a lift to Shirley's flat, and offered to take me home, but suddenly I decided no!! I said I had to wait for my parents and he laughed and looked hurt, and I jumped out of the Rolls and said goodbye — Oh Tash it's upset me! Especially as he said he actually called into RADA last Tuesday but I wasn't there — Godinheaven — its all wrong — still the only thing to do is not to think about it.

Six

HANNAH APPLIED TO the Royal Academy of Dramatic Art in the autumn of 1952. She was just sixteen, and her application form is filled out in childish block capitals. 'I have passed 4 subjects at O level and hope to obtain A levels in English Lit and History in July,' she wrote. The form is signed by my grandfather, as next of kin, and the headmaster, as 'Referee for Character and Respectability'.

I read this in the library at RADA, which still holds her file from fifty-five years ago. From this I learn that, because of her age, she was initially admitted to the Preparatory Academy, or PARADA, before being moved up after a term to the main school. I have always assumed that she graduated, but a pair of letters show that she left after a year, rather than the two needed to complete her studies.

In the first, dated September 1954, she wrote to give notice for the end of term. 'My English teacher at school always warned me that being the person that I was the stage would never be intellectually satisfying for me. I now am beginning to realise that he was quite right. I am afraid that I have expressed all this very badly. The truth is that the feeling of vocation has completely left me.'

A week later, she wrote to say that she was leaving right away. She had been for an interview at the Institut Français and been told that she needed to start immediately. She didn't say what she planned to do there, but 'the choice is out of my hands'.

THE STORY I HAD HEARD about Hannah at RADA was that she played the lead in Shakespeare opposite Albert Finney and Peter O'Toole. When I spoke to my father while writing my article, I asked if he remembered which play it was, and he said he thought it was *Twelfth Night*, with Hannah playing Viola, and either Finney or O'Toole as Sir Toby Belch.

But on the sheet in Hannah's file listing the plays in which she performed there is no mention of *Twelfth Night*. The only Shakespeare is *A Midsummer Night's Dream* — or 'The Dream' as it is listed — and Hannah played not Titania, the fairy queen, but two minor male parts, Puck, the king's jester, and Snug, the joiner, who plays the part of the lion in the play within the play.

The librarian confirms that Finney and O'Toole were at RADA at the same time as Hannah, though they were a year ahead of her. I ask him whether there is any way of finding out if either of them was in 'The Dream' with Hannah, or in any of the other plays on her sheet. He goes away into a back room and returns a few minutes later. Neither Finney nor O'Toole was in any of those plays.

FINNEY AND O'TOOLE are the only fellow students I have ever heard mentioned. The library has a list of Hannah's contemporaries, but there are hundreds of them, and I have no idea who might have been friendly with or would remember Hannah. The librarian suggests I speak to the alumni office, and a woman there offers to send a notice out with an alumni mailing. The only reply I get is from the actress Sylvia Syms, who writes that she didn't know Hannah, but that her own mother committed suicide when she was young, so she knows 'the mark it leaves on those left behind'. 'We will never know their reasons,' she adds.

ALTHOUGH MY FATHER knows what I am doing, he doesn't ask how my research is going, and the couple of times I try to ask him about Hannah it is uncomfortable for both of us. But one afternoon, when I am round at his house, he starts talking about Hannah — or at least about himself in relation to Hannah.

I know, from one of my grandmother's stories, that he and Hannah first met as children. Hannah, so the story goes, climbed a tree and wouldn't come down. I have always imagined that Hannah was nine or ten and my father fifteen or sixteen when this happened. But he tells me now that they were younger. It was during the war. Shirley's mother, his favourite aunt, was friends with Hannah's mother, and took him to Hannah's house somewhere out in the country. Amersham? I suggest. No, he says, something farm. Scarlett's Farm? That would have been the summer of 1940, when Hannah was three or four and he was nine. That sounds right, he says — and there is something about the idea of them meeting when they were so young that moves me again, and I sense that my father is moved, too, at the memory, though we do not say anything.

Instead he talks about the next time they met, at a fancy-dress party, when Hannah was seventeen and he had recently come down from Oxford. He had heard talk from his mother and aunt about the 'difficult' Fyvel girl, but as he had always been told by his mother that he was difficult, that didn't put him off — if anything, it made Hannah more intriguing.

There was a band, and he asked Hannah to dance. He had learned to dance on his national service in the army, in Berlin, during the airlift. His sergeant-major's wife had been the south-west England ballroom dancing champion, and because her husband didn't dance she taught my father the foxtrot and the quickstep, and he was her partner at the dances in the sergeants' mess.

He had a girlfriend from Oxford, a very nice girl. Her aunt ran a hotel in Bermuda, and invited her to come out for a year and work there, and she came to my father and asked him whether he thought she should take up the offer. She was asking, he thought, whether they were serious, whether they were going to get married. Before he met Hannah he might have told her to stay, but now he told her he thought she should go — it was an opportunity she shouldn't pass up.

Hannah was at RADA, by then, and when I ask him if he can think of anyone who was there with her, he says, or seems to say, Lady Bear; though what he is actually saying, he explains, is Lady, or Diana, Baer, or Diana Robinson as she was at RADA.

He still sees her socially, he says, saw her just the other day in fact, which disconcerts me, though of course he cannot avoid bumping into people who were friends with Hannah. He has lived with this all these years, this world of ghosts. It is new only for me.

DIANA BAER STARTED at PARADA at the same time as Hannah, she says, when I go to see her in Kensington. She loved it there. It was her first time out of school.

She shows me some photographs. They are of young people dressed up in period costumes on stage — though none is Hannah. She talks about movement lessons, voice projection, breathing. I ask about Hannah. She doesn't think Hannah ever really wanted to be an actress, she says. She talked incessantly about my father. She can't tell me any more, but she suggests I speak to another RADA friend, Sue Westerley-Smith, and when I get home I call her.

Sue was also at PARADA, which was in Highgate — a short

walk from the house where we were living when Hannah died. It was very old-fashioned. There was a daily assembly, which Hannah decided was too much like school. Sue remembers Hannah 'sitting at the back on a window sill playing cards'. 'I adored her,' she says. 'She made me laugh.'

IT IS NOT MUCH, but I am learning to make do with fragments, to construct a whole out of pieces, like an archaeologist conjuring a jar out of a few shards.

Though perhaps I have always been doing this, have seen the world in this way since I was a boy imagining my mother out of the little I was allowed to know. My first novel was narrated by a man 'who spent most of my childhood at the edge of things, listening to my own thoughts, or talk I was not supposed to hear, piecing together the world like a forbidden jigsaw, the pieces stolen one by one'. It was set in Africa, before I was born, and I didn't think of it as my own story, though I see now see how much of myself I put into it, that it was not coincidence that the final act of the main narrative is the mother's suicide.

My subsequent two novels had little in subject to do with Hannah, but both are fragmented narratives, collections of half stories that are left for the reader to piece together, find some greater sense in.

A COUPLE OF FRAGMENTS:

1. SUSIE MENTIONS A RECORD Hannah made of herself reciting poems while she was at RADA. She says she listened to it again and again as a child.

I have some old cine films of our family, of Hannah, which I have put onto DVD and have been watching. But they are silent. I have

97

no tape of her voice, no idea what she sounded like, and for weeks afterwards I think about this record, mourn its disappearance, its loss.

2. MY FATHER SAID he met Hannah at a fancy-dress party, and I think of the email I received about Hannah as a 'ravishing Carmen' at a fancy-dress party. Could it have been the same party? I contact the woman who wrote it. She doesn't remember my father being there — though it was a joint party for her sister and a cousin of Shirley's, so it is quite possible he came. It was September 1953, shortly after Hannah turned seventeen and started at PARADA.

I ask my father, and though he can't remember whether this was the party, I decide that it must have been. I am pleased to have discovered the night that my parents met, or met again. I know from my daughters that it is one of the stories children like to hear, how their parents met, the moment their own lives began to take shape — and I am happy that I have identified my own beginnings.

IT HAS BECOME a little easier talking with my father, and he continues his story on two or three afternoons. He had studied law at Oxford, but when he came down he needed to earn some money, and the year Hannah was at RADA he taught Latin and history at a boarding school near Reading.

He and Hannah weren't a 'proper item' initially. She had 'other boys on the radar', including an Israeli boy called Mike she had met through Shirley, while he was having 'a passionate affair with the under matron at the school'. But as the year went on he would often drive down to London and pick her up from the RADA cloakroom, as Sue Westerley-Smith had remembered. He had a 'very nice pre-war sports car, a Wolseley Hornet Special', he says.

Hannah had signed up to go on a tour of Israel for the summer of

1954, but my father and Hannah were growing more serious. Hannah told my grandparents she didn't want to go, but they insisted — perhaps because they had paid for the trip, though my father suggests they also wanted her to have a break from him.

By chance, I discover that the novelist Elisabeth Russell Taylor was on the same tour. The party, she remembers, was made up mostly of 'young, rich, and uninteresting' girls. Elisabeth was a few years older and 'politically antagonistic to the privileged'. But Hannah was more interesting. She 'clearly didn't want to be on the trip' and was 'argumentative, contentious, and self-opinionated'.

She talked about marrying my father 'in a black dress with red roses'. She was 'a bit of a pain'. But Elisabeth also uses the word 'courageous' to describe her. Hannah wasn't prepared to behave the way women were supposed to behave, and Elisabeth felt she would 'do something substantial with her life'.

WHAT HANNAH DID on coming back from Israel was give up her place at RADA and decide to marry my father. An announcement of their engagement appeared in *The Times* that November. My father was now studying for the Bar and living with his parents in Hampstead Garden Suburb. Hannah was also at home in her parents' flat near Regents Park, though what she was doing is less clear.

I have put off reading my grandfather's diaries, but I can't defer it any longer, and early one morning I fly with an empty suitcase up to Edinburgh, where Susie has been storing the boxes of diaries in her cellar.

In his later years, I remember my grandfather keeping a brief daily journal in the kind of desk diaries that have a page for each week below a reproduction of a painting of flowers. These were often open on his desk, and I saw once that he had written in the same word, 'weltschmerz', for every day of the week. I asked what it meant, and he explained it was the German for world-weariness, or ennui, and grinned ruefully. But most of the older diaries, like the one I looked at when sorting through my grandparents' house, are thick ring-bound notebooks, a hundred sheets in each, filled with his dense scrawl. Susie spends the day teaching me to decipher it, and in the evening I fly home with some of the diaries, Susie bringing the rest later, and begin to work my way through them.

Apart from a volume covering a Fulbright fellowship to America in late 1951 and early 1952, though, the diaries don't begin until the mid-1950s. The only reference to Hannah before this is in the last page of the American diary, when he describes coming home to find his daughter a 'bright, self-centred child'.

Other than that, the first mention of Hannah is in March 1955, a few months before her wedding. He has had, he wrote, some 'exploratory conversations with Hannah about her future', though frustratingly he doesn't say more.

Hannah wrote to RADA that she was leaving to attend the Institut Français. I ask my father what she did there, and he says she took a French A level so she could apply to university. But while she did eventually go to university, that was two years later, and if she took French A level that year before her marriage, she doesn't seem even to have passed, which seems unlikely.

In my old house, where my stepmother still lives, I find a batch of letters from a friend of my father's who was living in Aden. 'Why has she given up the drama?' he wrote after Hannah came back from her Israel tour. 'Your influence or Israel's? What is she doing now? You can't be living in sin all the time.'

It is a question I ask, too — and to which I don't have an answer. She was young, in love, had a wedding to think about. But I find it hard to believe that she spent the nine months between giving up RADA and getting married planning her wedding. When you live for only twenty-nine years, each one of those years matters, and it bothers me that I don't know what she was doing during this time — or to think that she was doing not very much, wasting those precious months.

WHAT I DO HAVE from this period, or topping and tailing this period, are a pair of cine films: one, the wedding of Hannah's cousin Naomi in the summer of 1954; the other, her own wedding, a year later, in July 1955.

The first film begins with flickering scenes of people arriving at the synagogue, smiling and waving at the camera — among them, Susie and Naomi's young sister, Donna, both aged about ten, in pale-blue bridesmaids' dresses. Later, at the reception, the bride and the groom cut the cake and kiss. The camera takes in the guests, men in glasses with thick frames, large-chested women in elaborate hats, until it comes to a young woman in the act of throwing her head back to take a slug from a bottle. When she lowers the bottle she is revealed to be Hannah. Seeing the camera, she pokes her head towards it, closes her eyes, and bares her teeth in a wide, gurning grin.

Outside later for the family portraits, the camera pans over a family line-up: the two sets of parents, the bride, her veil blowing in the wind, and groom, until it comes to Hannah again. She is wearing a pale-blue dress, too, has a white posy in her hand, is also a bridesmaid. So briefly that a less conscientious observer might miss it, her head shoots forward, and she makes the same gurning grin.

IN THE SECOND FILM, the same old cars pull up in front of the synagogue, the same sort of Jewish people get out — in some cases, actually the same people, though this time when the groom appears it

101

is my father, boyish and toothy, in top hat and morning suit. He smiles at the camera and salutes and walks forward, taking off his hat as he passes the camera.

Other relatives appear: a round-faced Shirley, her sisters, her mother, my father's parents. And here now is Hannah, posing on the steps with my grandfather, her veil blowing in the wind this time, dressed not in black, as she had boasted to Elisabeth Russell Taylor, but in white. She is still only eighteen, but it is her wedding, and instead of gurning she smiles demurely.

Afterwards, on the synagogue steps with my father, she kisses him chastely, and then kisses him again, perhaps at the request of a photographer, and this time they hold their kiss a little longer.

The film moves to the reception in a garden. My father has changed into a suit; Hannah is now in something black. Here, though not sitting together, are my grandmother and my grandfather, the father of the bride. He is young, still in his forties — the age I am now. He has undone the top button of his shirt, and his tie is flung over his shoulder. He holds up his hand to the camera, and smiles.

Spring 1954

Dear Tash, Received a phone call from Pop in the morning. Asked me to go out with him. Said I was going to Camb — he said I should cancel it. Nearly did then thought that I could have the best of both worlds by going out with him another day, he was rather annoyed but arranged to pick me up at RADA at 5pm following Thursday.

Went to Cambridge — felt very nervous. The cocktail party was very frightening at first, but I got invited by a rather nice boy to a Kings May Ball — I accepted it. (I'm not going — reason will be revealed below!)

Pop said he nearly didn't come as I didn't go out with him last Saturday. The evening was very nice, I like him more each time I see him. I think its much better to grow to like a person — much more secure. He asked me to come and live with him — (I declined.) I shan't go to the May Ball as I think he'll take me to an Oxford Commem! He says I'm the first girl he doesn't feel absolutely at ease with — because I haven't fallen head over heels etc. Says he thinks about me when with other girls.

P.S. Thought — difference between me and nice girls like Val — people ask her to marry them — people ask me to live with them.

Dear Tash, I often feel I lead a double life, for the world of the theatre is so complete, and all absorbing, that I find I change as I walk out of RADA to go home, or see Shirley etc.

I have been out with Pop several times since I last wrote. He really is very nice — (horrid word!) On Sunday I'm going down to visit him at the school where he is teaching. We get on together very well, and understand each other completely. He really is terribly sweet to me. We are going to two Commems on consecutive nights next month which ought to be bliss. Every time I see him I like him a little more — so far I hope none of the 'gang' (damn them) know. I can't bear being talked about.

Dear Tash, I had a blissful time on Wed evening we went (you know who the other half of we is) and had a super supper in a Chinese Restaurant and then went to a lovely Jazz Club called the Fauburg. It really is quite Parisienne and has a gorgeous bar I drank glasses of Coca Cola and Rum which is heaven and everything was ----! (I've run out of adjectives.)

Dear Tash, He's such bliss — we went to a wonderful party given by a girlfriend in Cirencester — her father owns a real dream house — tucked in the heart of the hills 7 miles into the country — with Rose gardens and a wonderful yew walk. That was last Saturday on Sunday I drove the car back to Oxford (its utter heaven driving an open car I went up to 70 mph once) and we took a punt on the river and slept for the whole afternoon.

I have told him about K — I had to because he had told me everything and it became a barrier between us — but he was wonderfully understanding & I love him.

Seven

THEY DROVE DOWN to the south of France for their honeymoon — in a Standard Eight, my father says, more at ease talking about his car than about Hannah. Back in London, they rented a flat off the King's Road. It was away from north London, where their families lived, but that was the attraction. My father had passed his Bar exams, but he didn't have the money, or the patience perhaps, to build up a barrister's practice, and the previous autumn he had started working for a printing firm in Soho, owned by the husband of a cousin. I have heard the story of this job before: how on his first day he was handed a broom and told to start sweeping; how within a couple of years he was running the company.

By the time they moved to Chelsea, he had been promoted to sales director and was earning a good salary. At the weekends, he and Hannah would drive out of London to stay at places like the New Inn in Winchelsea, on the East Sussex coast. That first winter they went skiing in Courchevel. There are photographs of them on the slopes, on lifts, with a skier in a bear costume, dancing in a bar.

The following spring, he bought a half-interest in a sailing boat that they kept at Dell Quay in West Sussex — a few miles from where he and my stepmother would later buy our barn. A man who lived in a hut on the foreshore looked after the boat, he remembers, for two and sixpence a week.

What he doesn't remember about these times, any more than in the year before they were married, is how Hannah filled her days. He was working hard to build up the business, he says, so that was where his thoughts were concentrated. But in the archives of Bedford College, the part of London University where she would eventually study, I find a clue. 'Left school at seventeen and married almost at once,' a note in her file says. 'Trained as a shorthand typist in order to supplement her husband's earnings. Her husband has had an unexpected promotion and she is now free to enter a university, which she has always wished to do.'

Secretarial school is the last place I would have expected to find Hannah, but when I ask my father, he says it 'rings a bell', though 'it certainly wasn't to supplement my income'. He suggests it might have been at my grandmother's suggestion, and points out that I did a typing course myself, though that was for three weeks, and because I wanted to be a journalist.

It is my father's wife who comes up with a suggestion. Hannah was newly married, and in the months after the wedding she would have been learning how to shop, cook, wash, iron, clean. She wouldn't have had the time or energy for anything more than a part-time secretarial course.

This still doesn't sound like the Hannah of my imagining, the author of *The Captive Wife*, until I remember a passport of Hannah's in which she had written her profession as 'Housewife'. Looking at it again, I check the date it was issued: a couple of weeks before her wedding. Had she applied for a new passport so she could go on honeymoon under her married name?

HER PERIOD AS HOUSEWIFE and shorthand typist did not, anyway, last long. Her application to Bedford College is dated February 1956, eight months after she was married. It was almost three years since she had left school, and, in comparison to her RADA application, her handwriting is smaller, neater, more grown-up. This time, the signature for her guardian is not her father's but her husband's. Asked to give his 'Profession or Business', my father wrote 'Barrister-at-Law', though he was working for a printing company rather than as a lawyer.

Hannah also practised a little untruth on the form — calling herself Hannah rather than Ann, her legal name, which has been written in on top by another hand. More seriously, letters in her file reveal that she altered the name on the copies of the exam certificates she sent in with her application.

She had 'always been known as Hannah', she wrote when her deceit was discovered, and 'it is my desire to use the name Hannah, which is why in the copy of the earlier certificates that I sent you, I substituted Hannah for Ann'.

The registrar wrote back that she had 'committed a serious misdemeanour', adding that he had 'some excuse for lacking confidence'. Fortunately he did not press the issue, beyond telling her that she would 'have to go through your University course with the name of Ann, even if you prefer the name of Hannah'.

It was, I am learning, a characteristic of Hannah: a disregard for rules, a sense, as with her driving on the pavement, that the normal codes of behaviour weren't for her. The story she told about my father's promotion freeing her to go to university was an understandable excuse for her lack of direction over the previous couple of years. But her file reveals that she also managed to finesse her way into Bedford. By the time she inquired about entrance, applications had closed, and she was told she would have to wait a year. Instead, the note in her file reveals, 'she called in to see Lady Williams', head of the sociology department.

Lady — or Professor Gertrude — Williams 'was not in

college', and instead Hannah was seen by a sociology lecturer, O. R. McGregor, to whom she told her story. She had come, she said, on 'the recommendation of Mr Mark Abrams', a well-known social statistician, who was a friend of my grandfather's and also, it seems, of Professor Williams's. Her name-dropping, along with her charm and intelligence, must have worked, for McGregor wrote that he was 'well impressed by her sensible outlook', and Hannah was allowed to sit the entrance exam, as long as she acquired a third A Level. (It was now, it seems, that she took and passed her French A level at the Institut Français.)

HANNAH BEGAN HER sociology degree at Bedford College — then an all-women's college on the edge of Regents Park — the following autumn, shortly after her twentieth birthday. She would study here for the next eight years, almost all the rest of her life, but I know nothing about her time at the college, other than that she got a first and wrote the thesis she would turn into *The Captive Wife*.

My father tells me he enjoyed reading the books Hannah brought home from Bedford, but he seldom went there. Nor can he think of any friends she made there, other than Anne Wicks, who I know, having looked her up early on, died of a cancer a few years ago. He does, though, mention Anne's husband, 'a rather nice chap' called Tony Wicks. He was an engineer, and my father had got him a job at his printing company. When Tony divorced Anne, he married someone else who worked there, and with this information I track him down.

Tony remembers, he says, Hannah's 'jet black hair, what I call Jewish hair'. Anne was 'a scholarship girl, from a poor family in Kent'. She was 'very bright, intense'. She started out in sociology but ended up in market research, which brought her into contact with 'media types, airy fairy types'. He was just 'a dull engineer', and they grew

110

apart. 'We just dissolved,' he says. 'No animosity, no settlement, no difficulties, nothing.'

He mentions a couple who lived in Primrose Hill who were close to Anne, but more interesting to me is another Bedford student he says was friendly with both Anne and Hannah. It takes me a while to find Erica, but when I do she tells me, 'I was remembering Hannah only the other day. She gave me a wooden salad bowl that I still have, and I think of her when I use it.'

Like Hannah, and Anne Wicks, Erica was a year or two older than most of the other students. Her home life had been difficult, and it had taken her a while to get herself to university. She met Hannah fairly early on and 'attached herself' to her. Hannah was very organised, and Erica often borrowed her notes.

Bedford College in the late 1950s was still very traditional. Erica lived in halls her first year, and the girls wore gowns for supper and had an evening curfew. Teaching was by lecture, though 'Hannah sometimes shouted out questions'. Erica also remembers making mischief with Anne and Hannah with the statistics lecturer. He was a good-looking young man, and the three women would sit in the front row of his lectures 'wearing low-cut tops, showing our cleavage'. He spoke without notes, walking up and down, and would splutter when he saw them.

She often had coffee with Hannah during the day, but she never saw her in the evenings. After her first year, Erica lived out of college and had a boyfriend at the Slade art college, and they would go out to jazz clubs, but Hannah always went home to my father. She sensed that it wasn't easy for Hannah trying to balance the different pieces of her life.

Despite this, Hannah did 'a great kindness to her'. In her third year at Bedford she became pregnant, and Hannah helped her with having

111

an abortion. This was still illegal in those days, and Hannah took her to the clinic and had her to stay for a few days while she recovered. 'Without your mother's help, I am not sure I would have finished my degree,' she says.

ERICA AND ANNE seem to have been Hannah's closest friends at Bedford, but in time I track down more of her contemporaries, and am even invited to a Bedford College reunion lunch. The common consensus is how innocent most of them were. Penelope Horsfall remembers the college putting on a fund-raiser for students in Hungary, and Hannah organising a skit for which the performers wore black trousers: it was the first time Penelope had ever put on trousers.

The teachers could be 'antediluvian'. One former student remembers O. R. McGregor, the lecturer who saw Hannah when she 'dropped by' the college, 'rocking back and forward on his heels during a lecture and telling the women in front of him, "You are all so mediocre."' McGregor, or 'Mac', and another lecturer would play ping-pong in the college, and when they 'slammed the ball down they would say the name of whichever student was bugging them'.

The women at the reunion lunch talk about how most of them ended up in caring careers of one sort or another — social work, citizen's advice, lady almoners. When they had children, almost all stopped working. Of the forty or so sociology students in Hannah's year, only three or four did research, and one of these gave up to get married, while another 'was kicked out when she got pregnant'.

Older, already married when she arrived, Hannah was 'different'. She had 'a film star's vitality, glamorous, and rather exotic'. And when she got pregnant in the first term of her second year, she had no intention either of getting rid of the baby or giving up her studies. In this she was fortunate in having the backing of Gertrude Williams, her head of department, who allowed her to extend her degree to four years, and wrote letters in support of her extending her grant. Her contemporaries remember Hannah bringing in her new baby in a little yellow romper suit. Hannah, who was twenty-one, was 'glowing with pride'.

SHE HAD BEEN EXPERIENCING minor gynaecological problems, my father tells me, and was advised that having a baby would cure them. Simon was born in Queen Charlotte's hospital in Hammersmith, on 23 April 1958, and spent his first months in the flat in Chelsea. Later that year, the new family moved back to north London, to the little modern house, on Hillside Gardens in Highgate, next door to the Kartuns, and close to both sets of grandparents.

The following spring they must have bought a cine camera, for the first family films are of Simon toddling around. With her bouffant hair and wide skirt, a cigarette in one hand while she hugs Simon with the other, Hannah looks like a suburban American housewife from a 1950s educational film.

This impression is repeated in the next reel, which shows her sewing in front of the house in Hillside Gardens, while Simon chases a kitten. In the next film, though, she looks slimmer, more stylish, even younger. In her black fitted shirt and tight dark-blue peddle-pushers, her hair more closely styled, she might now be a pretty young dancer from a Cliff Richard or Elvis Presley movie.

HILLSIDE GARDENS WAS one of a triangle of streets being redeveloped on the plot of an old mansion house that had fallen into disrepair and been knocked down. There was a communal garden in the middle and a communal atmosphere. Neighbours babysat for each other and shared school runs. The legacies of the war were finally being shaken

113

off, the early shoots of the new world that would blossom into the 1960s were beginning to emerge, and these affordable modern houses were attracting a forward-thinking brand of occupant.

Derek Kartun, for example, was a former foreign editor of the *Daily Worker* turned businessman — his company produced a 'fusible interlining' used in suits and uniforms — who would go on to write a series of spy thrillers. Paul Rogers, another resident of the triangle, was a film and stage actor who was the original Max in Harold Pinter's *The Homecoming*. Peter Jewell was an animal conservationist; his wife, Juliet Clutton-Brock, one of Britain's first archaeozoologists. Katrin Stroh was a developmental therapist. John Weeks was a modern architect. Cy Grant, a Guyanese musician, was the first black person to appear regularly on British television. Gillian Freeman's novel *The Leather Boys*, published in 1961, was the story of a relationship between two young homosexual men. Klaus Hinrichsen, who I knew as the proprietor of the toy shop on the Archway Road, was a champion of émigré German artists who had set up the 'Hutchison University' in the Isle of Man internment camp.

My father's job in the printing industry was rather stolid and old fashioned in comparison, though he was doing his best to liven it up. His success had come from recognising how rapidly the advertising industry was growing in Soho, where his company was by chance located. With his Oxford background — unusual for a printer — my father could relate to and even knew some of the young advertising copywriters and account executives. He bought extra presses, kept the factory running at night, and the business was soon booming.

In November 1959, a year after he and Hannah moved into Hillside Gardens, a trade magazine, the *British Printer*, published a profile of him under the headline, 'Espresso Age Printer'. Accompanying it is a photograph of my father sitting rather self-consciously on a windowsill in a stylishly cut suit, holding an African carved letter-opener in his hand. He is twenty-nine.

The way he comes across probably says as much about how he wanted to present himself as how he actually was. 'Gavron is relaxed in manner, serious and eclectic in his interests, with sociological and literary leanings. He is as critical of his times and as aware of their problems as anyone in his 20s, but his success leaves scant room for frustration and he is quite clearly no "angry young man".'

What he really wanted to be, he told the interviewer, was 'a motor racing driver'. He had decided against law because 'it was necessary to dress formally in black' and he 'came to the conclusion that he just wasn't formal by nature'. Taking up printing instead, 'he has risen with astonishing rapidity by linking his potential to the fortunes of a new kind of printing business'.

He, too, like his neighbours, was forging his way in the world, and if Hannah, one of the younger wives in the triangle, was still only a student, her husband's success, the lives unfolding around her, must have given her something to aspire to — a glimpse that her own road, with sociology itself blossoming as a discipline in the post-war era, might also take her somewhere new and exciting.

AMONG OUR NEIGHBOURS in Hillside Gardens, and again when both families moved into slightly larger modern houses, next door to each other, around the corner in Jacksons Lane, were the Weekses — John, the architect, and his wife, Barbara, and their two children, who were similar ages to Simon and me.

It is a long time since I have seen any of the Weekses, but my stepmother tells me that Barbara is still living in Jacksons Lane, and I cycle over and ring on the door. After a few moments, a window opens on the first floor, and a face I recognise looks out and says, 'Yes?'

When I tell her who I am, she stares at me as if I am a ghost. When she lets me in, I have a similar feeling about the interior. The houses in the row were all built identically, and walking up the slatted wooden stairs, my childhood fear of the gaps between them comes back to me. When Barbara directs me into the L-shaped sitting room, I feel I am in our old house. I don't remember Hannah, but I remember the night I woke and came down to find my father sitting under the stairs with the woman who would become my stepmother.

'We danced hand in hand across the road,' Barbara says of our two families moving into these houses. As we were now on the wrong side of the road for the communal garden, the parents knocked down the fence between the two back gardens and put up a climbing frame at the bottom, on which I remember playing. I remember, too, taking my first puff of a cigarette with Barbara's son in the alley beside our house. I can't have been older than six or seven.

Hannah was 'rather lovely and very spirited, always active', Barbara says. When Katrin Stroh locked herself out of her house, it was Hannah who climbed up the drainpipe and squeezed in through a window, though she was pregnant with me. She made Barbara promise not to tell my father.

Barbara reminds me, too, of something I have forgotten — that Hannah had a miscarriage between Simon and me, after seeing the film, *Psycho*.

When Barbara heard that Hannah was dead, her first thought was that it must have been a car crash. Hannah's driving had become more reckless in her last months. It wasn't only that she drove on the pavement; when Hannah did the school run, her children would tell Barbara about the latest incident.

She takes me upstairs to show me the bedrooms — the equivalents of the bunk room I shared with Simon, of Hannah's and my father's

116

room, where my father had sat Simon and me down the morning after her suicide to tell us that our mother was dead. My memory of that morning is so clear in my mind — the whiteness of the walls, the bedspread, the carpet, so like a cliché of a scene of rebirth — that I have always slightly distrusted it. But when I walk in to Barbara's bedroom, it is exactly as I have remembered it.

Later we walk across the road to the communal gardens. Cy Grant, the musician, used to lead the children around here at the summer parties, Barbara says, strumming on his guitar like the pied piper. I have no memory of this, or these gardens, but walking along the paths I feel a strange happiness.

Barbara points at the backs of houses, telling me who lives, or lived, in each one, until we come down a narrow path to the houses at the end of Hillside Gardens. The one we lived in is the very last. There is a little square of back garden and square windows leading into a little square sitting room.

'I was walking past once, and I saw your parents dancing together,' Barbara says. 'It was early evening, and it was still light, and your father was holding your mother, and they were doing some kind of ballroom dance.' She puts out her arm to show me, and curls her hand if she is holding someone by the waist.

'HANNAH AND POP [a family nickname for my father],' my grandfather wrote in his diary. 'How affectionate and loyal they are.'

Sonia told me how 'wrapped up' they were in each other. They had their own names for each other, their own banter. 'They were always cracking jokes,' Tasha said. 'It was as if they were trying to outbid each other.'

Nina Kidron, a friend from the last couple of years of Hannah's life, says it was 'an experience to be with them, like being with two

117

contenders in a game. Hannah would say something, and your dad would say no, that's not right, and she'd challenge him back. It was quite difficult for anyone else to keep up. Having dinner with them could be like watching a tennis match.'

They were 'two very strong personalities', according to my father's schoolfriend Roger Lavelle and his wife, Gunilla, who I meet one morning at a café in Highgate. Hannah spoke with 'such freedom', they say, which I take to mean that she didn't hold back. Gunilla remembers going shopping with Hannah, and how she switched the top and bottom on a swimming costume to get the right sizes for her. 'Everyone does it nowadays,' she says, 'but back then it was very daring — it would have been perceived as shoplifting.'

But they also talk about my parents' generosity. When Gunilla and Roger moved into their first house, they found a bottle of wine and a chicken casserole waiting for them; after Gunilla's first son was born, Hannah took her out.

I ask about Hannah's suicide, and they look at each other. 'We were busy with our own lives,' Gunilla says eventually. They hadn't seen Hannah much in her last year or two, 'but we felt we should have known there were troubles'.

They have never really discussed Hannah's death, even with each other. It was obvious that my father didn't want to talk about it, so they didn't either, 'out of loyalty to your father. We took the lead from him.'

All they can suggest is that Hannah was 'very proud', that she wouldn't have wanted to let people see that she was in trouble.

What they prefer to remember are the good times, such as the occasion when they went to a party in London with my father and Hannah, and found themselves somehow, magically, having breakfast the next morning in Brighton.

Date unknown

She was awake — her eyes open gazing at the ceiling which was stark disinfected hospital white. Of course, that's right, it had all started in the morning when she had been leaning over the fence in the back yard talking to Mrs Hope when suddenly she came over giddy and something inside her jerked rather painfully, and she felt sick, as the baby inside her made its first strong move to enter the world. She remembered Jim had been simply wonderful — it was a real stroke of luck, that just that morning he didn't have to be at the factory till 10.30am.

It was all going to be fine. That was until they got to the hospital and they told her that the kid wasn't doing what it should and they would have to operate. It wasn't as if she minded being cut open. But kids should be born as they were supposed to be.

Suddenly she realised what had happened. She had had a child her first her own child. Wonder whether its a boy or a girl, hope it's a girl.

'My baby where oh where is my baby.' The nurse looked grave but produced an efficient smile — your baby will be coming soon its a girl.

'Oh' wonderful relief. 'But why cant I see it now? Why isn't it here?'

'Your husband' the efficient smile said firmly. 'Your husband — he's waiting outside. I'll tell him to come in I'm sure you'd like to see him straight away.'

'Bella' he said taking both her hands. 'Bella dear.'

'Jim where's our baby where is our little girl?'

A look of anxiety was visible in Jims eyes — but was replaced almost immediately by a look of strong determination.

'Bella darling I want you to be very brave indeed.'

Hold on tight to his hands hold on tight so you cant fall, so you dont scream its dead as loud as you can.

'No its not dead but our baby is not made quite as it ought to be. You see Bella its bodys all right, fine in fact, its just that, well you see it has two heads.'

Eight

IN NOVEMBER 1959, after several episodes of back pain, my father had an operation to fuse two vertebrae in his spine. He was in hospital for six weeks, and had to learn to walk again, but Hannah, he makes a point of telling me, was at his bedside every day. 'Hannah rising to the occasion,' my grandfather wrote in his diary. 'Calm, efficient, cooperative: all the grumbling, unpleasant, egotistical side of her character has disappeared.'

The following summer, she got her first — 'one of only two in the whole university out of a total of over 130 students', my grandfather noted proudly in his diary. A couple of months later, she was back at Bedford College to start work on her PhD. She was soon also reviewing books, first for the *Daily Herald*, and later for the *Economist*, *New Society*, and other publications. On top of this, that autumn she became pregnant with me.

I HAVE BEEN going back regularly to my old house — now my stepmother's house — looking for Hannah material. I have brought home books, photographs, cine films, the sack of cups and rosettes, letters from my father's friend. My stepmother has also talked about some papers she saved when she came to live with us, though she has no idea where she put them. She hates to throw anything away, for which I am grateful, but it also means that it is difficult to find anything in the overflowing cupboards and stacks of boxes. I wander the house, looking in places I have already looked. Trying a rusty old filing cabinet again, I tug harder at a drawer and it comes out a little further, and at the back I see a wad of papers.

I take them out and spread them on the carpet, looking for a diary or notebook, though there is nothing like that. Much of the material seems to be returned cheques, receipts, papers to do with moving house, a travel itinerary. But there is also a sheet of paper with doodles of horses — Hannah still, it seems, kept a place in her heart for horses. There is a folder, too, of correspondence with her publishers. And a few letters, notes really, in her own hand, as well as one or two in my father's. And there is something else in her own hand: a rough draft of a story about a woman giving birth to a baby with two heads.

There is no date on the story, and I don't have enough of her handwriting to try to date it that way. But it seems likely that she wrote it around the time she was having children herself, perhaps during one of her pregnancies. When she was pregnant with Simon she was living in a flat, whereas with me she was in the house in Hillside Gardens, with a fence over which she could lean to talk to the neighbours, as in the story. By the time she had me she had also had the experience of giving birth in a 'stark disinfected' hospital room.

Does this story express her worries about having another child at the still young age of twenty-four? She had a full-time nanny, but full-time meant the hours during the week when she was at college, or the library, or conducting the ninety-six interviews with young mothers (she was aiming at one hundred, but ran out of steam) that were the basis of her thesis and the book it would become. In the evenings and at weekends, she was responsible for Simon, as well as running the house, cooking, making sure my father's shirts were ironed. Did the

124

baby with two heads represent the two demanding children she would have, or perhaps her competing selves of mother/wife and working/studying woman?

THE ANTIPATHY THE STORY expresses towards having a baby in hospital is more easily understood — these were the days when maternity wards were the domain of imperious male doctors and bossily efficient midwives — and was solved by having me at home. The story I have always been told is that I was delivered by an independent midwife who was later struck off, though it is only now that I wonder whether there was an underlying message to this. That Hannah was a careless mother. That she didn't look after me properly from the start. That, as my brother once said to me, we were probably better off without her.

The midwife, I discover, was called Erna Wright. I can't find anything about her being struck off, though by the late 1960s she had given up midwifery to open an Austrian restaurant in Camden Town, and she later trained as an aromatherapist. But she also published a landmark book, *The New Midwifery*, promoting the 'Lamaze' method of training for childbirth, which encouraged women to take control of the process, and was, according to her obituary in the *Guardian*, 'a catalyst for the development of natural childbirth' in Britain.

As it was, neither Hannah nor I seem to have been harmed by the experience. 'An easy birth, weighing 9 lbs and arriving in this world in 20 minutes,' my grandfather wrote in his diary. If I had been born in hospital, Hannah would probably have been kept in bed for a week, but at home she was up and about much sooner. When I was four days old, my grandfather recorded 'a pleasant supper' with Hannah and my father. A few days after this, her friend Phyllis Willmott wrote of giving a party and Hannah coming 'practically from her confinement — her second baby was born eight days ago'.

125

FOR PHYLL, she tells me when I go to see her, Hannah's rising so quickly from her birth bed was an example of the way she was trying to live, her desire to be in control of her body and fate — if it was also 'pushing it a bit'.

Hannah and Phyll had met when Hannah sought out Phyll's husband, the sociologist Peter Willmott, for advice about her thesis. Phyll speaks of both admiring Hannah and being 'immediately a little jealous' of her. Hannah came round to their house, and she and Peter were soon deep in talk. 'Hannah seemed so much more confident than I was,' she says, and even after they became friends, Phyll 'always had the feeling that I wasn't quite on the same plane as her'.

There was 'this growing feeling in the early Sixties that, as women, we should be taking on more responsibility for ourselves', she explains. 'It was difficult, working mothers were disapproved of, most of us didn't make the most of our lives, but Hannah seemed determined to do so. She was in advance of the pack, she was trying to break down the barriers against women.'

A FEW MONTHS after I was born, Hannah must have spoken to a reporter from the *Evening Standard*, for a diary item in the newspaper in December 1961 records her own views on the balance between her work and family, or at least how she presented these to a journalist:

Twenty-five-year-old company director's wife Hannah Gavron has solved the career-versus-baby problem very well. She has a three-year-old and a baby of four months. Yet with the aid of a daily nanny from 9.30 to 5.30 each weekday she has managed to take a first in sociology at London University and embark on a thesis. 'I've compromised as I'd have had an awful guilt neurosis if I'd handed Simon and Jeremy over completely,' she

126

said. 'I put them to bed every night and do all Saturday and Sunday. I don't mind Simon thinking he has two mothers. He seems quite secure and happy.'

Hannah wanted to be, to be seen to be, in full control of her life, Gunilla Lavelle said. But the story of the two-headed baby isn't the only clue to suggest that this wasn't always entirely the case. A couple of weeks before I was born, my grandfather wrote in his diary of finding Hannah 'in difficulties re her review. Retyped it for her.' A few months later, he noted his concerns about her attempts to mould the family to her needs. 'She is chafing at restrictions on her free time. To keep free in the evenings, she tries to force Jeremy into three feeds a day. He cries — this means effort: she is tired, irritable with Simon.'

I also have a chance meeting with a woman who tells me that she was my 'daytime minder' for a brief period when I was three, between our nanny leaving and our au pair girl starting. She talks about me being naughty and 'tipping over my breakfast and laughing'. Hannah, she says, 'was always rushing in and out of the house in a hurry'.

WHAT HANNAH WAS rushing to in the first couple of years of my life were her studies and research, her ninety-six interviews, for her thesis on 'the conflicts of housebound mothers', as she would later subtitle her book.

Looking back from our own times, the subject seems an obvious one, still relevant today, but in 1960 it was neither obvious nor easy for her to get past her academic supervisors. For all the advances gained by the suffragette movement, and the opportunities the war had given women to work and experience life beyond the family, the woman's movement was in retreat in the 1950s and early 1960s. In the post-war period, emphasis had been put on the role of motherhood in rebuilding

Britain. The Beveridge Report, the basis for social reforms, spoke of how 'housewives as mothers have vital work to do in ensuring the adequate continuance of the British race and of British ideals in the world'.

Women's magazines of this period similarly lauded the family. 'Women were no longer shown, as they had been in the stories published between the wars, as career pioneers, or as the patriotic activist of the Second World War,' Jessica Mann writes in *The Fifties Mystique*. All the post-war 'fictional heroines ever wanted to have was a husband, children and a pretty house'.

Even social science seemed to support this. Parenting experts like John Bowlby and Donald Winnicott preached the importance of the presence of mothers to their children. In 1958, the year my brother was born, Bowlby produced a pamphlet in which he warned that motherhood is 'scamped at one's peril'.

When Hannah began her thesis in 1960, Katharine Whitehorn's famous article about 'sluts' in the *Observer*, which challenged the idea of the perfect mother, was still three years away; as was the publication of Betty Friedan's *The Feminine Mystique*, which would have much less impact in Britain than in America. The resurgence of the women's movement proper was almost a decade away.

Sheila Rowbotham, one of the most eloquent proponents and historians of that movement, writes that, to young women at that time, feminism meant 'shadowy figures in long old-fashioned clothes who were somehow connected to the headmistresses who said you shouldn't wear high heels and make-up. It was all very prim and stiff and mainly concerned with keeping you away from boys.'

As a sociology student, Hannah might have come across isolated work from the 1950s, such as Viola Klein's papers on working wives. Perhaps she was inspired by the setting up in April 1960 — just as she was finishing her undergraduate degree — of the Housebound Wives Register, whose aim was to put isolated housewives in touch with each other. It may be she was also influenced by her father's strong moral worldview, the books he had written about a shared Palestine and racial equality. But it seems likely that there was also a personal element — that, for all her privileges of class and money, her choice of subject was in part a response to her own experiences, the stresses of balancing her studies with being a wife, a mother, a woman, an individual.

HER BEDFORD FILE shows it took her time both to find her title and get it approved. Her first proposal was tentative — a study of young mothers 'to see how far the social and economic changes affecting the status of women are giving rise to new marital and family patterns' — and even this met resistance. A note in her file informed her that her proposal 'has not been approved in its present form and you should discuss it with your supervisor before submitting another title for consideration on the enclosed form'. But her determination to continue is also recorded: 'On McGregor's advice she is withdrawing her application for the DSJR [Department for Social Justice and Regeneration] grant, on the grounds that she is unwilling to change the subject of her research which would not be acceptable to the DSJR.'

Once she got past these obstacles and began her interviews, her focus grew clearer. By early 1962, she had a more specific title: 'The position and opportunities of young mothers — progress or retrogression. (A study of the difficulties confronting young mothers in the contemporary family based on a comparative study of working class and middle class mothers.)'

Her interviewees were provided by a doctor friend's general practice in Kentish Town. Her interviewing technique, she recorded, was fluid, her aims qualitative rather than statistical, the emphasis placed on 'presenting a critical picture of the lives of these families rather than a rigid piece of scientific construction'. The thesis was soon progressing well. She may have had to give up her application for a DSJR grant, but she was awarded a postgraduate scholarship in her first year, and the choice of two in her second. 'Interviewing completed, now writing up thesis,' her supervisor, Ronald Fletcher, wrote in a brief report towards the end of 1962. 'Very good work.'

THE STRAINS IN HANNAH's domestic life after I was born also seem to have soon receded. In my first appearance in the family cine films, when I was a few weeks old, a smiling Hannah tickles me and then picks me up and pats my bottom. The camera, presumably in my father's hands, pans slowly up her body, admiring her slender legs in shorts, her stomach showing no sign of having given birth, as if taking pleasure in how quickly she has regained her figure.

In the next film, the following spring, I am larger, fatter, sitting in a high chair in the garden in a coat. A few months later, we are on a summer holiday in the south of France. Simon is swimming in a pair of yellow armbands. My father carries me into the sea in his arms. Later, Hannah appears, in a bathing suit in a garden, and sticks out her tongue at the camera.

AMONG THE ITEMS Susie brought down from Edinburgh is a copy of an American magazine, *Business Week*, dated summer 1962, which has a series of photographs of us from what I realise are this same holiday. The pictures illustrate an article about European businesses providing holiday villas for their executives. I don't know how the magazine came to choose my family, but the black-and-white photographs and quaint captions speak, as must have been the intention, of a young, happy, successful family, at a good time in the century.

Here are my father and Hannah being served lunch by the maid in the villa, with French cheese, a baguette, and a bottle of wine on the table in front of them. Here are the four of us in an open-top sports car — I am sitting on Hannah's lap in the front seat — 'off for sights of smart St Tropez'. Here are my parents dancing rather self-consciously in what looks like a cellar — 'Night life at St Tropez means twisting in one of the record night clubs.'

IN OCTOBER 1962, my grandfather wrote that Hannah had 'written four book reviews and one article'. Her writing must have improved, as his complaint was no longer that he had to help her but that she was doing her reviews 'without telling me'. She had also made her first appearance as a pundit on television. 'Still inexperienced, talking too fast,' my grandfather, an experienced broadcaster, noted in his diary. 'But when she smiles she lights up the screen.'

As a family, too, we were going up in the world. Towards the end of 1963 we moved round the corner from Hillside Gardens into a larger house on Jacksons Lane. My father had been working for a couple of years on a business deal, and in September 1964 he quit his cousin-in-law's firm and, with a loan from the city, bought a printing company. My father 'has pulled it off', my grandfather wrote in his diary. 'Hannah helped in introductions, helped in deal.'

HANNAH WAS ALSO now working. In August 1963, my grandfather noted, 'H gains position as lecturer in sociology at Hornsey College. £1600 a year!'

The only people I know about from Hannah's Hornsey days are the man with whom she had her affair, whose name I have learned is John Hayes, and David Page, who wrote the letter I so liked. I have come a long way since I last wrote to David Page, and I try him again, and this time he invites me to visit him in his Norfolk farmhouse. He meets me at his local train station, and on the drive he explains that Hannah taught not sociology at Hornsey but general studies, on a course he partly ran. He talks about the Coldstream Report of 1960, which established that art colleges had to give their students a liberal arts as well as a fine arts education: he and Hannah were both employed under this new policy.

While he makes tea, he lets me look at his appointments diary from Hannah's first year at Hornsey. Leafing through, I see records of classes she gave on Freud and psychology, the American civil war, the sociology/psychology of violence.

Like other art colleges, he tells me, when he comes back, Hornsey was expanding rapidly in the 1960s. The building where he and Hannah taught was shared with a primary school — during classes, children would fling pellets through the windows from the playground. The new Hornsey was a mix of the conservative and the more radical. One teacher, an Austrian-Jewish refugee, was famous for shouting at anyone who espoused left-wing views, 'If zat is what you sink, go and live in Moscow.' But there were also younger, more progressive, teachers — among them, Jonathan Miller, Michael Kidron, and Tom Nairn.

I ask about John Hayes, but David didn't know him well. He prefers to talk about Hannah, how popular with her students she was — with him, too. She was 'very much the new woman. In your face, a lot of cursing, smoking her cheroots. Anything a man could do she could, too.'

'To me, she was the epitome of a certain kind of life force,' he says. 'She lit the lamps when she walked in.' He shakes his head. 'I can't see how you can suppress that enough to do what she did.' He had felt

132

angry with her afterwards, he says. He was her friend. Why hadn't she come and talked to him?

HE SUGGESTS I CONTACT two Hornsey students who married each other. John Rickets and Norma Jacobs haven't moved far from Hornsey, and in their house in Muswell Hill they talk wistfully about their years at the college. John grew up on a council estate in Chingford, and going to Hornsey was 'a complete eye-opener'. The world of his childhood had been 'claustrophobic and tame and held down, and suddenly at Hornsey there was this freedom to think and be creative'.

Hannah seemed 'very sophisticated', but they could 'talk to her about anything'. Her classes were relaxed, students and teacher sitting in a circle. Norma remembers Hannah getting them to discuss how each of them was dressed, the images they were projecting. 'Nowadays that doesn't sound much,' she says, 'but at the time, thinking that way was a revelation to me.'

Hannah was on the advisory board of the student magazine, *Horn*, which they also both worked on, and John goes off to find some copies. These could not be more different from the staid college magazines I leafed through in the Bedford College archives. The artwork is 1960s psychedelic. There is a photograph of David Page wearing only a bowler hat and a fig leaf, and a cartoon drawing of the 'Horn machine', a multi-storied tractor-like vehicle, carrying everyone who worked on the magazine, including Hannah, clearly identifiable in miniskirt, thigh-length boots, and Mary Quant hairstyle.

Hornsey was the place to be in the 1960s, they say. The Rolling Stones and Cream played in the college bar. Ray Davies of the Kinks was a fellow student, and Rod Stewart was often found around the college, though he wasn't a student. Dave Clark of the Dave Clark Five had an uncle who was a caretaker at South Grove, and he used to hang around in the playground. 'The world was so conventional that it was easy to be revolutionary, but that didn't make it any less exciting,' they both seem to say at the same time. 'Anything was possible, there was everything to live for, and we were right in the middle of it.'

IT WAS ALSO THROUGH HORNSEY, I discover from her file of correspondence with her editor, that Hannah was introduced to her publishers, Routledge & Kegan Paul. The editor, Brian Southam, wrote to the college seeking someone to write an introduction to sociology for art students, and Hannah was suggested.

After a meeting in June 1964, Southam wrote to Hannah asking her for a proposal for the book. Stapled to his letter is a handwritten draft of Hannah's reply, edited in my father's hand. In front of her rather blunt beginning — 'Here is my proposal' — he has added, 'I also enjoyed our discussion and confirm that we have very much the same ideas about this book.'

Her proposal was forthright about her potential readers: 'My experience of teaching sociology to art students has revealed that they do not possess a wide vocabulary, that their general knowledge is limited, and that their interest has to be wooed.' But Southam replied that 'the Board was extremely impressed'. She was offered an advance of £100, and the contract was signed on 29 July.

There must also have been some discussion about Hannah's doctoral thesis, which she had by now completed, for three weeks later Southam wrote to say that he had received 'very favourable reports' on her typescript, and that Routledge would like to publish this as well.

IN OCTOBER 1964, a year after Hannah started working at Hornsey, my grandfather wrote in his diary: 'Hannah changing. Exotic looking: black hair straightened, red dress, brown skin. Has come up with a title

134

for her book, The Captive Wife.'

From the outside, life could scarcely have been better. My father's business was an exciting opportunity. Hannah was employed at Hornsey, with not one but two books commissioned. Simon was at school and I would soon be following, with the freedoms this gave my parents. We no longer needed a full-time nanny, and at the beginning of 1965 we got an au pair girl instead. Hannah and my father were still only twenty-eight and thirty-four respectively.

The cheques they wrote in the spring and summer of 1965 — returned, as cancelled cheques were in those days by the bank, and saved by my stepmother — give a vivid picture of the prosperous life they were rising into: Royal Opera House, Box Office Royal Court, Harrods, Heals, Selfridges, Deans Place Hotel, J. F. Lambie Savile Row tailor, as well as Peter Coxon Typing Services, Marie Stopes Memorial Clinic, and the Hornsey Labour Party

That summer we holidayed again in the south of France, this time for the whole of August, though my father returned to London a couple of times for work. The itinerary from the travel agent reveals that we took my father's car, a convertible Aston Martin DB4, and a thirteen-foot motor boat he had bought — a returned cheque records — for £639 13s. At Southend, car and boat were driven into the bulbous nose of a British United Air Ferries Carvair aeroplane, and we flew to Calais, where we spent the night in a hotel before catching a car train the following evening from Boulogne to St Raphael.

We were renting the upper floor of a villa in the Quartier Bellevue in La Croix Valmer. 'The flat is gorgeous, we have a marvellous view of the sea and it is very quiet,' Hannah wrote in the one letter to my grandparents that has survived. 'We are leading a nice feckless life, not tying ourselves down to any routine which is lovely! We are already quite brown and the kids look very well.'

135

Friends came to stay, including a friend of my father's and his male partner, and Anne Wicks, now separated from Tony, with her new boyfriend, Ghriam.

In contrast to three years earlier, there is only a minute or so of cine film, and a single roll of photographs from our month in France. Perhaps this was simply camera fatigue, though perhaps it hints at something else: a loosening of ties, at least in Hannah's mind, to the family portrayed here.

The cine film shows my brother and me leaping happily in the waves, our skin nut-brown, the water sparkling with sunlight. Later we are building a castle on the beach with my father, who kneels on the sand, fit and muscled.

Hannah must have been behind the camera for these scenes, but at the end there are a few seconds of her walking down the beach in a flimsy bikini. She is thinner than before. Her new haircut is hidden under a flowery bathing cap.

Pausing at the edge of the water, she starts to wave away the camera, but thinks better of it and turns the motion of her hand into a wave. She says something the silent film does not catch, and steps gingerly into the sea.

January 1965

We have a great many friends in their forties — I don't feel they have a great advantage in knowledge or experience. It's hard to say why — I suppose it springs from confidence in my ability to get any information if needed.

No one spends a lifetime any more working on a single subject.

It's of course hard to know what to tell my son about what happened in Germany during the war.

Our generation knows nothing of the period when Communist parties played an important part in Europe and were full of intellectuals — when I read that crummy book, *The Mandarins*, about how Sartre was angry with Camus and so on — it means nothing.

Do you notice how at the University unions they're constantly putting up provocative motions — that this house wants more contraception, or something — to attract notice and they're usually defeated. The young technicians are too busy acquiring their little car.

Early marriage also militates against rebelliousness.

Less class distinction, less race distinction, less conformism, less bad art — we're all for the right things if for the wrong motives often.

When I saw *Look Back in Anger* — we wandered into the second night by accident — I felt Osborne stood for us, he said all the things we had been saying.

138

The affirmative thing about the Victorians was that if they felt badly about a thing, they got up and said 'change it'. They still could make a fuss and change things the way we can't any more, from the lunacy laws to women's rights — just think of all the women pioneers; they had a sense of mission, of power, and used it.

Too much notice is taken of the opinion of artists.

Intellectuals are no use to anybody today: you've got to have something, to be a scientist, a physicist. Just ideas are no good any more: you need the machinery to carry them into effect.

Nine

I HAVE BEEN MEANING to get in touch with Jeanie, our au pair girl from Hannah's time, but have put it off for some reason, and when I call her in Sussex her husband says she is out and they are leaving for France for a month tomorrow. A month seems an unbearably long time, now that I have finally made contact, and I start to say that I could drive down this afternoon, but he stops me. Jeanie is in London, seeing their granddaughter. He gives me her mobile number, and when I call it turns out she is about to drop her granddaughter at nursery school a couple of miles from where I live, and we agree to meet at a café.

Jeanie stayed on with us for a couple of years after Hannah's death, and kept in touch with us through my childhood, but the only time we have met in the last twenty-five or more years was at Simon's funeral — though I recognised her immediately then, and felt an instinctive warmth towards her.

When I cycle up now to the café and see her sitting outside, I feel that same warmth, though something sadder and more yearnful rises in me, too. Perhaps these feelings, the association of Jeanie with those lost times, with my original family, are what has held me back me from contacting her until now.

We hug a little awkwardly — she does not look much different to me, but I have to remind myself that I am no longer the small boy she looked after.

She was, she says, scarcely more than a child herself when she came to us: she turned seventeen the day she started with us, on 4 February 1965.

She had answered an advertisement in the *Lady*, for a mother's help rather than an au pair girl. She can still remember her interview. I was playing with a plastic sword and I hit Hannah, and Jeanie was surprised by how patient Hannah was with me, scolding me gently. Her father was a colour sergeant in the Welsh Guards, and in her house 'you would have been given a clout for doing that'.

I was a 'little bundle of emotions', she says, while Simon was easier to handle, and she admits that she was more drawn to him at first. 'I wouldn't say this if Simon was still alive,' she says, 'but a few weeks after I arrived, Hannah told me she'd picked up that I felt closer to Simon. She said she was really glad that I had that closeness with him, because she felt closer to you.'

It is the story I have heard before, that I haven't believed, but I have no reason to doubt Jeanie's words. Though when I say it would explain why Simon always seemed so angry with me, she is surprised. Simon wasn't always angry with me, she says; he loved me, was protective of me.

She points to the little scar on my lip, asks if I remember how I got it, and when I say I don't, she tells me that it was in the playground in Highgate Wood, not long after she started with us. We were there with some friends and their au pair girl, Jeanie's friend, Sheila. I was sitting on a seesaw and Simon was rocking it, and I bounced forward too sharply and split my lip on the handle.

There was a lot of blood, and in her worry Jeanie told Simon off for rocking me too hard, and he burst into tears. He was 'mortified', she says, and he kept saying that he would never hurt me on purpose.

I am pleased to have learned the scar's origin, though I feel something more poignant, too. These are the kind of stories one usually hears from a parent — the kind that my daughters love hearing about their younger years. It is part of what binds us as a family, this shared past, these remembered experiences.

I think of a recent conversation at my father's table. We were talking about the nicknames we give our children, and my father was explaining the name his mother gave him. It occurred to me with a little flutter of excitement that perhaps Hannah had a name for me. But when I asked, the table grew quiet. My father looked flustered. He didn't remember, he said.

I suppose, I say to Jeanie, that it was after Hannah's death that the troubles between Simon and me started, but Jeanie denies this, too. Even after Hannah died, Simon was kind to me, she says, would help me pack my bag if he were going somewhere, would calm me down when I got upset.

She talks, too, about how she grew to be 'really so fond' of me, how she always gave me 'lots of kisses and cuddles', and I think of my instinctive warmth for her.

Later, memories of Simon will come back to me: of the time he lent me his patched jeans and platform boots to go to my first teenage party, of other acts of generosity when we were older that I found hard to reciprocate; though, also, the threat in his powerful arms, his fists, his gritted teeth.

Could it have been after Jeanie left that things deteriorated between us?

'HANNAH WAS DIFFERENT from anyone I had met before,' Jeanie says. The days Hannah worked at home, she would come downstairs at mid-morning and make coffee in a percolator on the stove and stir a spoonful of cream into two cups, which they would drink at the kitchen counter. Hannah would ask Jeanie about her life, or talk to her about the world, 'trying to bring me on a bit'.

Jeanie was amazed by the 'risqué things' Hannah would say. 'Smacks of bondage,' Hannah said of the title of her book — *The Captive Wife*. When my father's mother died, in May 1965, and Jeanie tried to offer her condolences, Hannah told her, 'It's alright, you don't have to express sympathy to me. In all honesty, I didn't like the woman, and she didn't like me.'

She remembers a song Hannah used to sing to me — 'Jeremy Jo has a mouth like an O and a wheelbarrow full of surprises'— and I get excited, I know this song, I must remember Hannah singing it to me, until I realise why I know it. It is an A. A. Milne poem, 'Jonathan Jo'. I have read it to my daughters.

She talks about our holiday to France that last summer. She remembers us finding a dead eel on the beach, and how Hannah and my father joked about who was going to give it 'bouche à bouche'.

She remembers how we would 'motor' on the boat to different bays for lunch and to swim on the beaches, singing the Beatles' 'Ticket to Ride'. Hannah would sit astride the bow in her bikini to keep the nose down and help the boat plane. One day we started back late, and the wind picked up, and my father had to bring the boat home through choppy waves and failing light. It was an anxious trip, but by the time we were safely home, the experience had become another adventure.

She remembers Hannah taking her shopping in the market in St Tropez. This was where to find the latest fashions before they hit

Carnaby Street, Hannah told her. They each bought T-shirts and hipster trousers, and Hannah bought a little denim peaked cap I have seen her wearing in photographs.

She remembers Hannah sunbathing on the balcony and my father standing in front of her, and Hannah saying, 'When you block my sun it's lucky I love you.'

She didn't know about Hannah's affair then, but looking back she can see there were tensions in the air, especially when Anne Wicks came to stay. She thought at the time that this was because my father didn't like Anne, though later she wondered if things might have been said, or hinted at.

EARLIER THAT YEAR, shortly before Jeanie arrived, my grandfather had interviewed Hannah for a book he was writing on intellectuals, and though there is no record of his questions, among his papers is the typescript of her answers.

Her comments show her to be articulate and opinionated. But what to make of the confident assertions about Sartre or the Victorians, the sweeping dismissals of artists, students, technicians? She was talking to her father, of course, wasn't taking the consideration she might have done with someone else, was perhaps even playing up to him. But her words remind me how young she was, how sure of themselves the young can be, how quick to make decisions about things.

Her dismissal of intellectuals is surprising, as an academic herself, with an intellectual book of her own in the making. Though perhaps she was expressing an anxiety that her ideas wouldn't be heard, that she wouldn't be able to change things like the Victorian women pioneers she spoke about.

Since the excitement of the previous summer, when Routledge & Kegan Paul had given her a contract for one book, and agreed to

145

publish her thesis as another, her academic progress had stalled in several ways. She had finished her thesis by mid-1964, but in early 1965 she was still waiting to discover if it had been approved — and until it was, the publishers were holding back on the contract for *The Captive Wife*. On top of this, she had also applied for two academic posts at the London School of Economics, and had failed to get either.

The delay in awarding her doctorate seems to have been more cock-up than conspiracy. 'To Hannah's distress,' my grandfather would write later, her supervisor, Ronald Fletcher, 'kept the thesis lying about with masculine sloth for half a year in 1964–5.' Susie also remembers Hannah sending Fletcher a telegram saying, 'Worried you are using my thesis for lavatory paper.'

But a couple of enigmatic entries in my grandfather's diaries hint that there might have been something more freighted in her rejections from the LSE. '"Lightweight." I was angry,' my grandfather noted after the second rejection. And a few weeks later, he wrote of O. R. McGregor, a lecturer when Hannah started at Bedford, but by 1964 a professor and head of the sociology department, and therefore likely to have written Hannah's references: 'definitely the enemy'.

What exactly he meant by this is unclear, but the suggestion that Hannah, in her work on the situation of women, was perhaps running up against male opposition, is supported by a story I have heard from Susan Downes's husband, David Downes, who was a young lecturer at the LSE when Hannah applied.

David had met Hannah through Susan, and was 'chuffed' when he heard she might be coming to the LSE. After her interview, he asked Professor Richard Titmuss, the doyen of social policy at the LSE, who had chaired her interview board, how it had gone, and was told only that Hannah had 'worn too much green eye make-up'.

146

IN APRIL 1965, though, Hannah was finally awarded her doctorate. 'We are all naturally delighted,' my grandmother wrote to her sister Zelda in Israel. 'It is a great relief to her.' This must have been shortly after I cut open my lip, for she went on, 'Jeremy is fine. The accident has left him with only a small scar on his lip and his teeth haven't fallen out.' A couple of weeks later my grandfather wrote in his diary that Hannah had signed her contract for *The Captive Wife*.

As far as my grandfather was concerned, Hannah's troubles were resolved. She was 'writing her Intro to Sociology'. My father had recently made some money by selling shares. 'Their success,' my grandfather concluded with satisfaction.

In mid-June, he wrote of attending a party given by Hannah and my father, perhaps to celebrate their tenth wedding anniversary. 'How many people they know. Everybody!' My father, he wrote, was 'calm and confident'. Hannah was 'v friendly: sense she is now central figure in family'.

It was his other daughter, Susie, who was causing him worry. In January, Susie had announced her engagement to her boyfriend, a young Cambridge don. But in March, Susie told my grandparents 'she does not want to marry him. Not yet. Cold feet.' And in April, she had run off with another man. When she came back, there was an 'evening of emotion'.

Towards the end of June, Susie was causing worry again, and my grandfather turned to Hannah for advice: 'Hannah's reassurance: Susie is tough.'

A few weeks later, we left for our month in France. In mid-August, my grandfather wrote of seeing my father on one of his flying trips back to London for work: 'brown, fit, confident'. In early September, with all of us back, he recorded a 'pleasant' walk on Primrose Hill with Simon and me. Later that month, Hannah helped him with his book.

147

'Enjoyed it!' he noted.

And then, a few days later:

October 4: 'bombshell — H, other man. Cold feeling in belly.'

October 6: My father 'cannot bear it passively. Threatens to cut off Hannah, wants to keep her, his self-esteem. I try to calm him, say: play for time.'

October 7: 'They to see a psychiatrist. M [my grandmother]: ring now. She does! Fix appointment!'

October 8: 'Highgate. Find the Gavrons much more cheerful. For moment — all held back.'

October 14: 'Hannah telephones. Ominous, again. Hannah has seen lawyer. The children neglected. I feel — disaster.'

October 19: 'M from call box'. My father 'has left'.

JEANIE REMEMBERS my father coming downstairs that morning with a couple of suitcases, and Hannah saying something about him going on a business trip, though later, over their morning coffee, she told Jeanie that things had been difficult between them and that they needed a bit of space.

My father stayed at first at the Ritz. Later, he moved into a muse house behind Harley Street owned by a doctor friend. Jeanie remembers him coming to see Simon and me in the evenings.

Hannah didn't confide directly in Jeanie about her affair with John Hayes, but she talked about a colleague who had been homosexual but was now seeing a woman. 'She never told me the woman was her,' Jeanie remembers, 'but after a while I worked out that it must be.'

ON THE AFTERNOON of my father's departure, my grandfather wrote that Hannah was 'cautious, controlled, determined. Tells me her side.' My father was 'impossible to live with! Fighting for her identity as an individual. His determination to dominate. I am being talked round as we sit there — on H's side.'

But that evening my father visited my grandparents. Hannah was 'pushing him towards declaring divorce', but he suggested a 'trial separation'. 'Hannah could draw cheques, run the house, see her John. Must see a psychiatrist.' After this, my grandfather's 'heart — and head — warmed to him. Now I'm on his side.'

In the morning, Hannah came round to my grandparents' house to hear my father's terms. 'She agrees, wearily, half-green,' but 'demurs at psychiatrist'. She will 'see her John — but not in the house'.

Afterwards she drove my grandfather to his office in Bush House — 'like a lunatic — disregarding traffic — a psychopath's drive — my hair stands on end'.

RATHER THAN A PSYCHIATRIST, Hannah went to Sussex University to see an old friend, Tony Ryle, whose general practice in Kentish Town had supplied her with the interviewees for her thesis, and was now the campus doctor.

'Tony Ryle has helped,' my grandfather recorded when Hannah returned from Sussex on 27 October. A 'truce' between Hannah and my father. 'Two dominant characters. They'll go to Tavistock counsellors.'

If, by this, my grandfather meant marriage-guidance counsellors, the talk was in fact now of them seeing a well-known psychiatrist, Anthony Storr. 'Now what about Storr do you really want to go or are my parents pushing you?' Hannah wrote to my father. 'I will go willingly if it is your wish. Let me know what you want and whether you wish to arrange it for me. We are all as well as can be expected. I hope it is not too awful for you. I think of you constantly and worry all the time.'

'If you would go to Storr I would appreciate it,' my father wrote in return. 'I suggest you make your appointments and I make mine.'

My father has no memory of seeing Anthony Storr, though early in 1966 he wrote out a cheque to him for £12 12s, the charge for two appointments. On 12 December, two days before her death, Hannah wrote a cheque to David Malan, another psychiatrist, to whom Anthony Storr seems to have referred her. Her cheque was for £6 6s — the charge for one appointment.

Anthony Storr is long dead, but David Malan is still alive. Would he remember what was said in a single consultation almost fifty years ago? I am tantalised by this thought, as I am by the thought of the notes he would have taken. But he is old and unwell, and my attempts to contact him are firmly rebuffed.

For what was said in those consultations I have only my father's memory that Hannah was told that there was nothing wrong with her, that she was going through an ordinary life crisis. That and a letter of condolence from Anthony Storr, in which he said it was 'tragic' that Hannah 'was not able to accept the help she was offered' — whatever that means.

ON 30 OCTOBER, Susie married her fiancé in Cambridge. The guests were the two sets of parents and the groom's brother. Hannah was invited, but she told Susie that she couldn't come, as 'things were too complicated'.

Hannah was still at Hornsey, but she had handed in her resignation and was looking again for a more serious academic post. Her visit to Tony Ryle seems to have given her an idea, for early in November my grandfather wrote a letter to a friend at the University of Sussex, inquiring about sociology posts, though this doesn't seem to have yielded anything. Five days later, he wrote in his diary, 'Depressing: H no job, no core I think. Confused. I feel sad for her.'

She had finished proofreading *The Captive Wife*, and was eager for it to come out. She wrote to Brian Southam at Routledge 'that she would do anything to avoid delaying' publication. The 'vital date to beat is Christmas'.

Why Christmas? Her concern surely wasn't to get it into the bookshops in time for the seasonal rush. *The Captive Wife*, for all the attention it would get, was hardly a stocking filler. More likely, perhaps, is that she was hoping that the publication of the book might help her find a job.

As it was, the publishers scheduled *The Captive Wife* for the following spring, and it was the other book she was supposed to be writing that Southam was more immediately concerned about. 'Our production department is wondering about the Introduction to Sociology,' he wrote on 5 November. 'I wonder if you can let me have a note of its progress and a likely date of delivery.' It is the last letter in her file of correspondence with the publishers.

'HANNAH, ADRIFT!' my grandfather wrote soon after. 'The house dirty — Jean — uncertain. Whither?' A week later, he wrote of Hannah telling my father: 'return, let's try. Can't promise more.' My grandfather was 'enormously relieved'.

But two days later, an 'early telephone from H. Final break. Not bearable.'

THROUGH ALL THIS, Hannah continued to fulfill her teaching duties at Hornsey, and even took up other work. In the last two weeks of her life, her bank statements record that she was paid £31 10s for acting as a jurist for students' work at the Architectural Association, £8 8s for book reviews from the *Economist*, and £6 6s from the BBC for her contribution to a radio feature on *Women at Work*.

On 2 December, my grandfather wrote in his diary that Hannah had finally secured a job: 'at the Institute of Education. £2000 a year and a secretary. With Basil Bernstein — plus endless prospects.'

He didn't say what the job was, but it would probably have been a mix of research, perhaps on the sociology of education, and supervising graduate students. The institute didn't teach undergraduates, it wasn't the LSE, but it was a prestigious establishment, and Basil Bernstein was a rising star.

'Dec 5,' my grandfather's diary records. 'Hannah for supper. Slowly she thaws. Talks of her new job.'

The following Saturday, 11 December, Hannah seems to have gone shopping for clothes, for among her returned cheques is one made out to Zing Boutique for £2 12s. Perhaps she wanted an outfit to impress her new boss, for on the Sunday evening she went to supper with Basil Bernstein and his psychologist wife, Marion, at the home of Donald MacRae, a supportive older sociologist.

'She spent Sunday evening with us and won the instant admiration of our daughters,' Donald MacRae would write to my grandfather later. 'She seemed to look forward to her work at the Institute, and when she left we all felt that it had been a happy evening. Marion and Basil Bernstein shared our feelings for her and felt as we did.'

The next evening, Monday 13 December, Hannah visited my grandparents. She was 'cheerful', my grandfather wrote. My father was being 'more flexible, much nicer', and Hannah seems to have suggested she was cooling on John Hayes, for my grandfather wrote hopefully of my father having a chance with her, 'if he plays a long shot, since there is no other man on the scene'.

THE FOLLOWING MORNING, Tuesday 14 December 1965, Hannah phoned through an order to a grocery shop in Highgate village, as she often did, to save time in her busy schedule. The groceries were delivered an hour or two later, and Jeanie unpacked them as usual — though not so usual was the half bottle of vodka she found in the box. In the year she had been with the family, drink had always been ordered from a wine merchants', and when Jeanie put the half bottle on the sideboard she noticed a bottle of vodka already there, still almost full.

It was the last day of my term, my last day at nursery school, and there was a Christmas party in the afternoon. When it was time for Hannah to take me, she told Jeanie that she wasn't sure when she would be back, and asked Jeanie to collect me. Jeanie often picked me up from nursery school — it was only a few minutes' walk from our house. But she thought it strange that Hannah hadn't said where she was going or what time she would be home. Hannah always told Jeanie what she was doing, and was never late. It was how she was able to manage all the different parts of her life, by keeping to a schedule.

After Hannah and I had left, Jeanie set about cleaning the kitchen and sitting room. She wasn't the most enthusiastic cleaner, and a few months earlier she had overheard Hannah discussing her attitude with my father. He had advised Hannah to 'give her hell', but instead Hannah had raised her pay by ten shillings a week, to encourage her to try a little harder.

Dusting now, Jeanie tried to concentrate, but coming around the corner from the kitchen into the sitting room she noticed that the half bottle of vodka she had left on the sideboard was missing. It could only have been Hannah who had taken it, and it planted another seed of doubt in Jeanie's mind. What would Hannah be doing with a half bottle of vodka?

Jeanie picked me up a couple of hours later. She had grown used to me, 'had grown fond' of me, but I was still a handful, and took up most of her attention. Even so, she couldn't stop thinking about the vodka and Hannah's failure to say when she would be home; and when her friend Sheila phoned later, she mentioned it to her. Sheila dismissed her worries. It was Christmas, Hannah was probably going to a party at the art college. That was why she had taken the vodka and why she didn't know when she'd be back.

Sheila's explanation was reasonable, but Jeanie's worries continued to play on her mind, especially when the neighbour, Barbara Weeks, brought Simon back from school, and the afternoon darkened into evening, and Hannah was still not home.

From *Six Days in January*, by Arnold Wesker, 1966–67

The door of the café was abruptly opened and a slim young woman entered; she seemed to have opened the wrong door, but then resigned herself as though every door she opened would be the wrong one. At first she was uncertain whether to stay, and then appeared sorry to have made the decision to come at all. Her coat was of brown suede, sombre and severely cut, with a high mandarin neckline, giving her the appearance of an earnest young commissar. It was only when you looked closely at her that you realized her eyes were mournful and not eager.

Katerina Levinson came to their table and smiled a slow, apologetic smile.

'I like the Hammersmith flyover, I hate the Shell building; I like the GPO tower, I hate the Roehampton flats'.

'Abroad. On business. I dumped the children with my mother and fled.'

'The whole bloody family weekend'.

'I see my friends cheated into engaging their large sensitivities upon the little music of insensitive young men who, when they've sung their pleasant songs, will disappear and leave nothing but a great confusion behind them. I see headlines about wars and famine which witness a relentlessly monumental stupidity from political leaders about which I can do nothing. I see my friends surrender to a facile image of themselves that countless magazines perpetrate — and you expect me to take courage because in the midst of it all they cook complicated meals and invent Christmas cards?'

'I'm sorry,' she said. 'I'm feeling very frail, as though an accident has given me so many bruises I can't bear the risk of more batterings, of any kind. And everything batters me. Harsh words. Foolish, stale, insensitive words. Ugly crockery, unlovely faces, obscene shaped furniture, monstrous buildings. Offensive. So much of it. Fraudulent, synthetic, I can't seem to take them any more, the offences. All of it, offensive. I flinch. I'm sorry, I daren't look at things for long. Don't you ever want to rush away from conversations on buses and trains. Voices hard and bony. Offensive. Ugh! And cruelty.'

'I don't want any more knowledge of pain, I — I want — I'm sorry.'

Ten

THE DOORBELL RANG in my grandparents' house at around five o'clock that afternoon. It was Anne Wicks. She had come home to her flat in Chalcot Square to find the police there. When they explained what had happened, she walked the two hundred yards to my grandparents' house in Chalcot Crescent to tell them.

It is fifteen years since I opened my grandfather's diary from that day and dropped it back into its box as if it might burn my hands — and it is no easier now to read the words he wrote that evening. He usually wrote in blue biro, but his entry recording his daughter's death is in red, the letters three times their normal size, as if their colour and shape could express the horror that the words could not convey, could draw out of him some of his pain.

After phoning my father, he took a taxi to University College Hospital, where Hannah had been taken. 'The faintest hope — artificial respiration?' he wrote. 'No hope. Dead. In the ambulance, said the doctor. I go to see.'

Jeanie remembers my grandmother and father arriving at our house and going upstairs to Simon and me, though they could not bring themselves to tell us that evening and we were put to bed. Later, my father came down and told Jeanie he had some bad news, and Jeanie, who had been holding that uneasy feeling inside her all afternoon, asked if it was Hannah, whether it was a car accident, which didn't make sense of her earlier worries but was all she could imagine.

My father didn't correct her, nor did my grandparents. It was only at the inquest that Jeanie learned that Hannah had killed herself. As far as she remembers, though she stayed with us for two more years, my father never spoke Hannah's name in her presence again.

He did say she should come into the sitting room to be with him and my grandparents, though soon afterwards my grandmother suggested she go to see her friend Sheila. She remembers running through the streets to Sheila's house.

My grandfather wrote of friends and family gathering at our house as the evening drew on. At one point, my father said, 'What are we waiting for? Nothing is going to happen.' At another, the phone rang, and my father picked it up, listened for a moment, and said, 'She's dead,' and hung up.

THE NEXT DAY, my grandfather drove to St Pancras coroner's offices to meet 'a friendly investigator'. 'I put my cards on the table,' he wrote in his diary. My father 'not there. Separation. Of course — she may have met someone at the flat.'

Though these weren't quite all his cards. He didn't reveal that he knew that Hannah had been having an affair, or that the man's name was John Hayes. In fact, he seems to have tried to suppress this information. He wrote of Anne Wicks telephoning him, 'angered at being asked to be reticent' — asked, presumably, not to say anything herself about John Hayes.

Jeanie, too, remembers mentioning the half bottle of vodka to my grandmother, and being advised that she 'didn't need to say anything about that at the inquest'.

What was the purpose of these concealments? To protect Hannah's reputation? To lessen the shame? Though perhaps it was simply to do something, to wrest some small control of a situation in which any meaningful ability to influence events had been taken from them.

HANNAH'S INQUEST TOOK PLACE two days after her death, on Thursday 16 December, at the St Pancras coroner's court — the same place where Sylvia Plath's inquest had been held two years earlier. 'The drab, damp coroner's court,' Al Alvarez wrote in his account of Plath's death in *The Savage God*.

My grandfather recorded in his diary that he swore his oath 'with a handkerchief' on his head, and told the court 'how nicely Hannah had spoken' of my father at his last meeting with her.

The coroner asked if he had ever 'feared she could do such a thing as commit suicide. The coroner's eyes rested on me. No — never imagined.'

Asked the same question, he noted, Anne Wicks replied, 'No — nothing crossed my mind.'

'The only possible verdict,' the coroner concluded, 'was that in a state of mind we cannot know Hannah Gavron deliberately and efficiently took her own life.'

THE FUNERAL WAS HELD that afternoon at Golders Green crematorium. My brother and I remained at home with our grandmother. There were five mourners: my two grandfathers, my father, Susie, and the family solicitor. 'Jews with caps bear the coffin,' my grandfather wrote. 'An organ plays. I weep and weep and weep.' If anyone spoke, he did not record it.

A couple of days later, my grandparents fled to Israel to stay with relatives; a day or two after that, my father took Simon, Jeanie, and me skiing with friends in Switzerland. My only memory of this holiday is that we were snowed in and I was excited by talk that we might have to fly out by helicopter — though in the end the snow must have cleared, for we left by train.

I HAVE ALWAYS KNOWN that Hannah was cremated, but it is only now that it occurs to me to wonder about her ashes. I have seen no mention of ashes in my grandfather's diary — and everything of importance went into his diaries. I ask Susie and my father, but they do not remember.

I call the crematorium. I am hoping only to learn what might have happened to her ashes, but the woman I speak to asks for Hannah's name, and tells me to hold. A couple of minutes later, she comes back. Records of ashes have been retained since 1962. Hannah's were kept for six months, she tells me, and were then, like all unclaimed ashes, spread on the crematorium lawns.

She asks for my address and a few days later a map arrives. Hannah's ashes were 'dispersed' on section 4-M of the memorial lawns, alongside the thorn bed by the east boundary wall.

A MONTH OR SO after Hannah died, my father received a letter from University College Hospital, asking him to collect 'some clothing and a watch which belonged to your wife'. I ask him about these items, but he doesn't remember whether he collected them. If he did, they were not kept. I have seen no watch of Hannah's, have seen her clothes only in photographs.

Jeanie, who spent those days 'tiptoeing around the house in silence, not knowing what to say', remembers that Hannah's clothes went quickly, presumably to charity. My grandmother asked her if she wanted anything, but Jeanie already had an anorak Hannah had given her, and she said this was enough.

162

Hannah's work papers went to my grandfather, his diary records, though they had gone, perhaps long before, by the time Susie and I sorted through his house.

Most of her jewelry disappeared, too, though when my brother got married my father produced Hannah's engagement ring from a bank security box. My brother gave it to his wife at the ceremony, but when she washed her hands later that day, the ring slipped off and disappeared down the plughole. The plumbing beneath was taken apart, but the ring was never found.

What happened to Hannah's wedding ring I do not know. Perhaps she took it off in those last weeks, and it disappeared with everything else. Or perhaps it was still on her finger when she died, and went missing at the hospital. The nanny who looked after Simon and me when we were small, who I looked after in the last years of her life, died in hospital, and her wedding ring, which she always wore, was not among the possessions returned to me. It may be that Hannah's wedding ring is sitting now on a stranger's ring finger.

IN ONE OF OUR AFTERNOON TALKS about Hannah, I summon the courage to ask my father about the way things were handled after her death — why so little of hers was kept, why we fell into such complete silence about her.

He doesn't remember her possessions being given or thrown away, he says, but he agrees that they must have been. He suggests that perhaps he felt it wasn't fair on my stepmother to be surrounded by signs of Hannah, though my stepmother has told me that most of Hannah's possessions had gone by the time she moved in with us, and it was she who saved the few papers that remained.

He mentions a child psychiatrist Simon and I were taken to see, how she advised that we were too young to be told that our mother had killed herself. He and my grandparents were worried that if they talked about Hannah we would ask questions, he says, that they wouldn't be able to keep the truth from us.

I understand the first part of this. I remember my own anxieties about telling Leah about Hannah. I have read, too, that Ted Hughes also tried to protect his young children from the bleak facts of their mother's death.

The second part — the silence, the putting away of all photographs, the clearing out of her possessions — is harder for me to understand. My grandmother kept some photographs of Hannah on display, told us her stories about Hannah. I have, too, a letter the psychiatrist wrote to my father about Simon in which she emphasised that 'in order that the mourning is satisfactorily accomplished it is very important for him to be able to think about his mother and face his grief'.

For as long as I can remember, my father's gaze has been directed at what lies ahead. He doesn't believe in worrying about the past, or lingering over problems that can't be solved. 'The arrival, not the journey,' is one of his sayings. 'A for achievement and E for effort,' is another. But how much is this his nature, and how much was he shaped by the events of that afternoon?

Had he never thought, I venture, of putting aside a few of Hannah's things for Simon and me, for when we were older, for when we might want to know more about her?

'The feeling was that the thing to do was to make a fresh start,' he says, as if he is talking about someone else's feelings, someone else's decisions.

'The feeling was,' he says again, 'that her book was the thing to keep. It was her achievement.'

He is almost eighty when we have this conversation. What does he see when he looks back across half a century? Does he recognise the man he was then? 'I was punch drunk for a long time afterwards,' he says. 'I was so off balance, I couldn't think about anything properly.'

THOUGH SO MUCH of Hannah's was discarded, both my grandparents and my father kept the letters of condolence they were sent after her death. These tell me little about Hannah, but seeing how wordless, helpless, the writers were rendered by her act helps me to understand a little more the need to turn away.

'There cannot be anything which I can do or write to be of any use,' reads a typical letter. 'One would write a lot but at such a time feelings rise above words,' goes another. 'I have to accept that news of this nature is not lightly put about,' wrote a third, 'though I find it almost impossible to believe.'

Even Anna Freud, at whose clinic in Hampstead my grandmother was now working, could write nothing more helpful than, 'I think I can feel the whole weight of it because I had a sister who died at the age of your daughter and also left two little children of the same age. We all tried to fill her place for the children, and the ups and downs of that struggle are very much on my mind.'

Few of the letter writers attempted to remember Hannah, to find solace in the death by celebrating aspects of the life, as letters of condolence conventionally do. How, seems to be their message, do you remember someone who erased herself? How do you mourn someone who so completely rejected you? How do you carry on your own life in the face of such a thing?

In *The Savage God*, his 1971 study of suicide, Al Alvarez wrote that after centuries in which suicide had been a mortal sin (suicides buried at crossroads with stakes through their hearts or stones over their faces), and a criminal offence (people were still being imprisoned in England

165

for attempted suicide until the late 1950s), suicide had become by the 1960s 'a private vice, another "dirty little secret", something shameful to be avoided and tidied away, unmentionable and faintly salacious, less self-slaughter than self-abuse'.

If words like 'little', 'tidied', and 'faintly' seem to me strangely evasive, as if Alvarez was writing of a suburban affair rather than the devastating legacy of the suicide of a young mother, the secrecy he writes about was certainly true in Hannah's case. Not one of the letters of condolence refers directly to the manner of Hannah's death, and only a few even hint at it.

The only letters that attempt to offer some understanding or consolation are from two of Hannah's childhood friends, Jill Steinberg and Sonia Jackson. 'I feel very much,' Jill wrote, 'that Hannah gave so many people so much help — she did more for her fellows in a very deep, real sense in such a short time, than most of us do in 60 years — that when the time came, she had nothing left for herself.'

'Wherever she was she was always the centre, throwing off sparks in every direction,' Sonia wrote. 'It's true about Hannah what Frieda said about [D.H.] Lawrence — she lived every moment of her life to the fullest possible extent. Perhaps you can't live at that pitch of intensity for seventy years.'

IN MAY 1966, six months after Hannah's death, *The Captive Wife* was finally published. It was a single-handed piece of research by a woman in her twenties, based on her doctoral thesis, and put out by an academic house, but the findings contained in its catchy title, that some women felt trapped and depressed rather than happy and satisfied at home with their children, were picked up by almost every newspaper and magazine, from the *Evening Standard* to the *Morning Star*, the women's magazine *Nova* to the *British Medical Journal*.

'Is Your Wife just a Bird in a Plastic Cage?' ran the headline in the *Sunday Express*, above a half-page article suggesting that, 'in terms of human happiness', *The Captive Wife* 'could be the most important book of 1966'. 'Is mother a nuisance?' asked a column in the *Daily Mail*. 'And if she isn't why does Britain insist on treating her like one?'

The *Observer* ran an extract from the book across its op-ed page, below a drawing of a woman looking through bars. The following week, most of the paper's letters were given over to responses, including one from a woman who wrote that her husband regarded her desire to work as 'an understandable wish, like wanting a holiday in Greece, but not as a need that society is under an obligation to notice', and signed herself, 'Another Captive Wife'.

This phrase was widely taken up. So many people were thinking about 'the captive wife', one article claimed, that 'far from being the most inconspicuous member of society, she is now one of the most controversial, sought after and discussed'. 'O Captive Wives, Belt Up!' ran another less sympathetic one.

Many of these articles acknowledged the 'untimely' or 'tragic' death of the book's young writer. But not one revealed how she had died, or asked, as newspapers surely would today, whether there might have been a connection between the subject of the book and the fate of its author.

In many cases, the writers of the articles wouldn't have known that she had killed herself. But at least some must have known. Her inquest had been reported in at least two local papers in north London, where many journalists and book reviewers lived. There was no internet, no texting or social media to disseminate gossip, but news still spread. The review in *New Society* was written by Donald MacRae, the sociologist who had hosted Hannah at a dinner two nights before her death, and whose letter of condolence to my grandfather made clear that he knew how she had died. But in his review he did not mention this. Silence, it seems, whether out of respect, or manners, or Alvarez's shameful avoiding and tidying away, was the natural response of the times.

MY GRANDFATHER EMPLOYED a cuttings agency to make sure he did not miss any references to his daughter, but the success of *The Captive Wife* seems only to have deepened his torment. 'If you had been alive,' he wrote in his diary, 'how you'd have enjoyed it! What might you have achieved?'

His diaries in the months after his daughter's death are agonising to read. He remembers 'her cold body in the mortuary. I stroked her brow. Should I have kissed her?' Everything is poignant. Leaving our house after a visit, he hears my father putting on the radio, and this simple domestic act overwhelms him. Things Simon and I do or say remind him of Hannah, but we are not Hannah, not 'substitutes'.

His diaries were mostly a receptacle for his despair, but here and there they chronicle his attempts to find some sense. He must have heard, perhaps from Anne Wicks when she came round to tell them that Hannah was dead, that there had been an argument with John Hayes, for early in January he recorded a talk with Susie, who told him that 'Hannah could not bear rejection'. He went over his memories of Hannah's visit on the evening before her death. She sat 'talking to me in detail' about her work, his work, my father, Susie. 'The only conclusion,' he decided, is that 'what happened had not been planned before Tuesday.'

On January 29, six weeks after Hannah's death, the doorbell of his house rang. It was Anne Wicks again, 'wanting to talk'.

168

He had written in his diaries of my father's anger with Anne Wicks. He noted now my grandmother's 'anguished face'. Fortunately, perhaps, Simon and I were there. 'Anne realises — it's awkward — steals away.' But my grandfather decided he needed to talk to Anne, and a week later he met her. 'Smiling. Young. Composed,' he wrote.

'There had been a row between Hannah and John Hayes,' she confirmed. Hannah 'wanted to rush John, a revolution in his life, but he didn't want to be rushed'. Hannah 'stormed out', but John 'did not think it final. They'll telephone, talk again.' But by the time John tried to make contact, it was too late.

Anne found him 'on her doorstep in evening. Hysterical. Had to be sedated by doctor.' He wanted to write to my grandparents, 'despairing apology, that too weak to help Hannah in her hour of need', but Anne had dissuaded him.

She suggested that there was no point in my grandfather meeting him. He would discover only 'a nice handsome affection-giving young man'. Anne had been 'utterly against her taking up with him', but Hannah would not listen.

My grandfather told her that my grandmother said there was 'no-one who such good brains and so little control on her emotions', and Anne 'agreed'.

Hannah had told Anne that if John rejected her she would kill herself, but she hadn't believed her. Hannah was, though, 'genuinely afraid of being alone — would be an old maid if John did not marry her — would find it difficult to find a man who'd take her on, a tough proposition, and she herself was choosy'.

Anthony Storr, the psychiatrist, had been 'hopeless', Anne said. She 'felt like writing him an angry letter'.

She had spent the first month 'with fantasies in which I was saving

169

Hannah — arguing with her'. 'Like myself,' my grandfather added.

'Not as much a villain' as my father suggested, he wrote. 'Saw her off.'

DESPITE ANNE WICKS's advice, my grandfather wrote to John Hayes, and a couple of weeks later the two men met for lunch at my grandfather's club.

'Young, nice looking. Recognised me,' my grandfather wrote. 'Yes — have a drink. A large double gin. We talk.'

'I discover: He ex Rochdale Grammar School. To Oriel, schoolmaster, now MA in sociology.'

My grandfather asked what Hannah wanted from him. 'Well, marriage and a declaration. To be married by Christmas, as a plan. She, only she, would make him into a whole human being.'

And the quarrel? 'Hannah wanted him to spend a night at Jacksons Lane. He, no — Jean, the kids. A 'semi quarrel'. Anyhow, Hannah stormed out. Angry.'

In the evening, 'since Hannah so angry', he had called her at home, intending 'to say that yes he would stay the next night. Only to find' my father 'answering' — presumably the call to which my father had said, 'She's dead,' and hung up.

From here on, my grandfather's notes are increasingly elliptical:

He wasn't ready — the children — afraid.

His 'nature'.

Had not suspected such action. Hannah joked: always carried sleeping pills, her poison.

Drove recklessly. Would laugh. Take life lightly.

I talk of her death. He breaks down. Weeps. I hold his hand.

I say goodbye to John Hayes. Bust. Shattered. So ordinary a boy.

'The mystery has deepened!' my grandfather wrote, and for me, too, these conversations raise more questions than they answer. Was Hannah really afraid at twenty-nine that she would be on the shelf if John Hayes didn't marry her? How exactly was Anthony Storr 'hopeless?' Why Christmas again? How come Hannah 'always carried sleeping pills'? And how did so apparently little add up to the decision to take her own life, to the act, the step, the leap, of doing so?

As far as my grandfather's diaries record, this was the end of his active efforts as a detective, though he continued to ask others for their opinions — provoking them, it almost seems, to unsympathetic judgements.

She 'was a narcissist', one female friend told him. 'Other people real to her only in the part they played. The whole enterprise with John was a fiction.'

'Were her feelings for other people limited?' asked his sister-in-law, Eva (who had made the comment about Hannah being clever in the hours after she was born). 'Must have been. If she left such burdens.'

'Oh my darling,' he added. 'I am aware that you could be ruthless.'

Susie's husband of a few months told him, 'Hannah so forceful — personality clear to him after only four meetings! We all only had walk on parts in her life.'

Another man whose name I don't recognise 'wants to talk about Hannah — he's had experience of suicidees. He says Hannah had few friends, found personal relations difficult. Did we know?'

He had lunch with Fred Warburg, his old publisher friend, who brought a message from his wife, Pamela. 'Hannah was always an outsider, unusual, solitary, and so on — she, Pamela, understood.'

In the months after Hannah's death, my grandfather began seeing a psychoanalyst, who 'probes and probes about Hannah' and concluded: 'A schizoid gifted young woman. I agree — schizoid.'

MY GRANDFATHER'S DIARIES were, I understand, not written to be read. They were a safe place for him to pour out his darkest thoughts. But reading these comments, I bristle. Who were these people, some of whom hardly knew Hannah, to decide she was a narcissist, had no friends, thought only of herself? Who was this psychoanalyst who diagnosed her after her death as 'schizoid'?

The word itself sounds like an insult. I look it up in the Oxford dictionary: 'Resembling or tending towards schizophrenia, but with milder or less developed symptoms; pertaining to or affected by a personality disorder marked by coldness and inability to form social relations.' Is this the Hannah I have heard about from friends like Tasha, Shirley, Carole Cutner, Erica, Gunilla Lavelle? Ambitious, strong-minded, dramatic, even selfish at times — but a personality disorder marked by coldness? Unable to form social relations?

Of all the friends my grandfather records talking to about Hannah, only one — Cherry Marshall — spoke with any softness and generosity towards Hannah, advised him to be understanding, forgiving.

Cherry told him how when she had herself fallen in love with a man outside her marriage, 'husband, children, work — all vanished. It was like catching a disease. Suddenly her life had a different point, it had not been fulfilled, it was a different drama entirely.'

'Be light on Hannah,' Cherry pleaded. 'Her passionate, hopeless love.'

'The intelligent woman is worse off,' she said. 'She can't cling, plead, blackmail, even console herself.'

This is the only one of these conversations I can read easily, but it seems, in its kindness, to have been the most difficult for my grandfather, to have stirred his pity, his guilt, for he wrote, 'The talk upset me terribly.'

GUILT IS ONE OF THE MOST devastating legacies of suicide. Phyll Willmott wrote in her diaries of her 'guilt that I did not do more, see more, understand the desperation of her state'. For my grandfather, his guilt must at times have been overwhelming. 'I had a wonderful daughter,' he castigated himself, 'and did not take proper care.'

The burden of his guilt explains, I think, why he was so ready to believe these harsh judgements of his daughter's character. In November 1966, he wrote how the prospect of a lunch he had arranged with Donald MacRae 'oppresses me. Perhaps meeting with all who loved H oppresses me.'

Remembering Hannah as his 'darling child, the most enchanting sprite ever', as he describes her once, was too upsetting. It was easier to think of her as fatally flawed, unable to control her emotions, schizoid. If there was something cracked inside her, then he couldn't have helped her, didn't need to feel so guilty.

In his diaries, he returns again and again to memories of her childhood melodramas, wilfulness:

'Aged 2, frantic with joy, too frantic to keep still.'

'Aged 4, we force her to give in, come to us. She cries, cries, then comes running, overborne.'

'You must have been six or seven, it was on the Edelmans' lawn, you played a game whereby Sonia and Natasha and another girl had to catch you and as they came at you from all sides suddenly you stood still and screamed — in panic. No way out?'

My grandmother's 'mother had died, the telegram had come, you were twelve or thirteen and going to London with your friend, and there was only one thing you wanted, to be away, while Susie comforted her mother'.

One of these memories — or rather memory of something he was told — is even the solitary reference to the headmaster in his diaries: 'Hannah, the story goes, hurt at 15–16 while skiing, assisted off by K with his arm around her — this leading to her affaire.'

From *What Are You Doing To Me*, T. R. Fyvel, 1950s

This overdue move to the larger house was demanded by the change in Desmond's practice.

Besides, precocious as she was, Ann would in a year or two probably start bringing young men to the house. Lucille frowned: this idea was like a small cloud, like an enemy infiltration.

Yes, Ann at fourteen was the one blot. Now John — of course he was younger — John was a perfect joy.

Lucille started. Echoing up the stair, intruding through the open door, came the opening chords of Chopin's Polonaise in B on the piano below. Then dead silence, and then a clear, overloud young voice.

'Mummy.'

Lucille stiffened, but held herself in restraint. Walking out to the landing, she called down in a quiet voice. 'What is it, Ann? You know how often I've asked you not to shout through the house.'

'Can I play the piano?'

'Really, my dear, must you? The packers will be here in half an hour.'

A pause. 'Mummy, you see moving is such a melancholy event and it's been raining all afternoon and I feel I simply must play some Chopin.'

Back in her room, she could feel how Ann's absurd phrase about melancholy had already disrupted her own mood of quiet recollection.

She sat down again and bent over the open drawer.

Heavens, how startling; how completely she had forgotten that it was there. Rollo, she thought: Rollo had gone off with the fellow to this garter ten years ago. For a few seconds Lucille sat very still. No, she had no real regrets about the three affaires which had punctuated her respectable married life.

And here — here was the series of family photographs.

Ann had carried on and yelled that she wanted to sit with her Daddy, as if in any such family portrait the proper place for a child was not on her mother's lap.

Lucille sighed. Why should she have been so unfairly singled out with such a difficult daughter?

She'd simply carried on patiently, whenever necessary, pointing out to Ann the faults in her character and showing her that if she persisted in treating other people without consideration only she herself would suffer, quite apart from spoiling what could be a lovely family life.

Ann, as tall as her mother and not unlike her, but at once paler and more vivid, and with the melodramatic air of fourteen about her entrance, stood breathless on the threshold.

'Oh let me see, what are those old photographs?'

'You see, darling, even at that age you were too egotistical. You see that's your main fault — egotism.'

'But what's this?' From the bottom of the drawer she pulled out a tiny pair of worn red shoes and held them up.

'Oh those?' Lucille herself looked at the shoes with surprise as she remembered. 'They are shoes you wore when you took your first steps.'

'Oh, Mummy, Mummy, how nice,' Ann exclaimed, dramatically rubbing her cheek against Lucille's.

John, strolling cheerfully into the room, surveyed the scene with a ten-year-old's matter of factness.

'I say, what are they in aid of?'

Lucille looked at him. With his school blazer and his apple cheeks he looked irresistible, she thought. 'Those baby shoes? You know, I made a funny mistake just now. I thought they were Ann's first shoes, but now I look at them carefully I see they're yours.'

Ann was already half way out of the room. Pale, young, beautiful, but with her assurance gone in a flash, she stood in the open doorway looking at her mother.

Eleven

DESPITE HIS FOCUS on the flaws in Hannah's personality, there is almost nothing in my grandfather's diaries about where these cracks might have come from, the influences, nature and nurture, that might have shaped her. It wasn't that these were matters beyond his understanding. He wrote knowledgeably about history, sociology, psychology. His wife was a devoted follower of Freud: Hannah was seen by a Freudian at the age of two. He was in psychoanalysis himself in the years after Hannah's death. He wrote both in an essay about his childhood and on several occasions in his diary about his own parents' influences on him. But with Hannah, I think it was territory he was simply unable to enter. It was burden enough to blame himself for failing her at the last; to imagine that he and my grandmother might have failed her as a child, that their own blood might have failed her, was more than he could allow himself to consider.

In all his diaries, there is only one moment when his mind leaps ahead of him through this forbidden door. In April 1970, four years after Hannah's death, news reached my grandparents of another sudden death in the family. My grandmother's younger sister, Zelda, had been suffering from bowel cancer, but seemed to have recovered after an operation when she was found dead. 'There was a strong suspicion,' their sister-in-law Eva informed them from Israel, that she had 'taken an overdose of sleeping pills with the intention of finishing it all'.

Zelda had returned to work, Eva wrote, but, while 'physically she was much better', her 'spirits were low and she kept on saying that she was terribly afraid of the whole thing starting all over again'. It must though have been 'a very sudden decision, because she had many appointments and meetings for the next few days'. A note, 'scribbled on an envelope in a large and hurried handwriting', said she had 'bad pain and have taken something to sleep. Don't disturb me.' She had 'enormous courage and tried her best to come back to life', Eva concluded. 'But underneath it all there was a deep despair.'

'How like Hannah,' my grandfather wrote in shocked recognition in his diary. 'The sudden decision! While plans pending! The hurried note on an envelope! In large, untidy writing! I feel a sense of cold undermining.'

But as abruptly as the door opened, it seems to have closed again. Reading on in his diaries, I find nothing further about these parallels, no suggestion that they might hint at a family trait. If he was to imagine that Hannah might be like her aunt, then he might have to ask whether she might be like her father.

Zelda's story, which I haven't heard before, is a jolt to me, though. On its own, for all the similarities with Hannah, Zelda's death does not necessarily add up to anything. It wasn't clear that Zelda took a deliberate overdose; her death may have been accidental. But the same cannot be said for her sister, Ruth, who also had bowel cancer, a decade or so after Zelda, also went into hospital for an operation, in Johannesburg, where she lived, and though the operation was also successful, climbed out of her hospital bed a few days later, took the gun she had smuggled in out of her bag, and shot herself dead.

MY GRANDPARENTS NEVER SPOKE to me about Ruth's death, and I learned her story only by chance. My grandfather had also stopped keeping a diary by the time Ruth died, in 1980, so there is no record of his thoughts about her death. Ruth's older daughter, Naomi, at whose wedding Hannah gurned at the camera, died from bowel cancer. But Ruth's younger daughter, Donna, lives in London.

I haven't seen Donna in a while, and when I call her and she invites me to her flat, I am taken aback to hear that she lives in Chalcot Square — where Anne Wicks's flat was. These past fifteen years I have lived myself only a couple of miles from here. My daughters went to nursery school a few streets away. One of my oldest friends lives almost around the corner. But it is only now, on the way to Donna's, that I go to see the house where my mother died.

In Hannah's time, this was a bohemian area, with most of the houses divided into inexpensive flats. But today it is one of the most expensive parts of north London, and Anne Wicks's address no longer exists. The basement flat she rented has been subsumed back into the grand mid-Victorian corner house, now a single family dwelling, with immaculate paintwork.

I stand at the glossy black railings and peer down at the basement windows. If Mr Popjoy, or one of his successors, was called to investigate a gas leak now, he wouldn't be able to get past the bars. I think about knocking on the front door, asking if I can have a look inside, but what would there be to see? And what would I say? Do the people who live here now want to hear about a young woman's suicide in their house?

INSTEAD I WALK across the square and ring on Donna's bell.

Donna knows, she tells me, that Hannah died here, though she doesn't know in which house, has never tried to find out — has never, if she is to be honest, given it much thought. She met Hannah when she came to London for Naomi's wedding, but she was only a girl then, and by the time she came back to London as an adult, Hannah was dead and no one talked about her. It was 'the great unsaid', she says, but then our family is 'full of great unsaids'.

Donna's own great unsaid was that she grew up believing her father was her mother's first husband, rather than, as was actually the case, the second husband, with whom Ruth had a long affair before they eventually married. She didn't, Donna says, want anyone to know that Donna was 'a bastard'.

It was only years later, in therapy in London, that Donna realised the truth. It was as if a 'blindness' had lifted from her. She went back to South Africa to confront the second husband, who admitted he was her father, though he begged her not to tell Ruth that she had found out, and Donna never did. It is 'the way we do things in our family', Donna says. Keep secrets, evade the truths we do not want to be true.

Donna was living in London when Ruth died, and though she was in her thirties by then, and was a mother herself, she was not told at first that Ruth had taken her own life. She was also persuaded not to return to South Africa for the funeral — something she has regretted ever since.

We talk about these evasions, Ruth's suicide, and Donna suggests that they are the same pattern of behaviour: a reluctance to deal with unpleasant things, whether the shame of infidelity or the indignities of cancer. Add to this a ruthlessness, too, perhaps, as my grandfather wrote of Hannah, a steeliness; for not every mother could keep up a lifelong lie to her daughter about her father, as not every seventy-year-old woman could take a gun into hospital and use it.

It was her second husband, Donna's father, who had given her the gun, Donna says. It was what everyone in South Africa had — affairs and guns.

A few days after Ruth's death, Donna received a letter from her. It had been written before she went into hospital, in case something happened in the operation room, or afterwards. 'I have decided "no tears",' Ruth wrote.

LATER, WHEN I TALK TO SUSIE about my conversation with Donna, she suggests that Ruth's and Zelda's might not have been the only suicides in the family. Their mother — Hannah's grandmother — Rosie, had suffered badly from 'melancholia'. She was in and out of sanatoriums, and was eventually sent to Switzerland, where she supposedly died of a heart attack while undergoing electro-convulsive therapy — though Susie thinks it is possible that she took her own life.

Rosie's husband, Nicolai, had no melancholy in his blood. He was known in South Africa, where he was chairman of the South Africa Zionist Federation, as Tsar Nicolai. After Rosie's death, Nicolai went to live in Israel where, according to an obituary, he spent the trial of Adolf Eichmann 'parading the streets of Jerusalem bearing a placard urging that the Holy Land should not be defiled by having the body of this arch-murderer interred in it'.

But there is also a story about Nicolai's death. As an old man, he came to London to have his throat cancer treated by a doctor who was well known, Susie says, for 'going to extra lengths'. According to the story, Nicolai instructed the doctor not to wake him from surgery if the cancer had spread. He died under the knife in July 1965, six months before Hannah.

THIS RELUCTANCE TO DEAL with unpleasant things, to put up with indignities, even the streak of ruthlessness, or steeliness, is something I knew in my grandmother. Although she was caring and generous, she refused to go to funerals — including her own daughter's. She was a loyal and forgiving friend up to a point, but if someone went beyond that point she would cut them out of her life. 'You are pushing me beyond my limit,' she would say about even small things.

She didn't commit suicide like her sisters, but she often talked about doing so when she got old or sick, and was for many years a member of the Voluntary Euthanasia Society. It wasn't death she feared, she would say, but the 'sordid paraphernalia of dying', and it was perhaps only the dementia she had always dreaded that prevented her choosing her own moment to slip away.

Is that how it was with Hannah? That she was taken beyond her limit? That she was not willing to put up with the indignities of a failed marriage, being rejected by her lover? It explains, and it does not explain. Ruth, Zelda, Rosie, Nicolai, were old, or at least a lot older than Hannah, and suffering from horrible illnesses. Hannah was twenty-nine and in perfect health. It is one thing to chose one's moment to slip away; another, to cut short a life in youthful bloom.

IN THESE CONVERSATIONS about family history, other matters come up, too. The proclivity for infidelity, for instance. Ruth, Zelda, Susie tells me — Nicolai, too, she thinks — all had extra-marital affairs. My grandfather's father, Berthold Feiwel, who has a street named after him in Tel Aviv for his contribution to Zionism, was also notorious for his philandering. My grandparents, too, had affairs: my grandmother with a man she would take up with when she visited South Africa, Susie tells me, and my grandfather when he was away in the war and on his travels. I remember myself walking with my grandparents in New York, and my grandfather, in his seventies by then, pointing to a hotel and asking mischievously whether he should tell my grandmother about the woman he had slept with there.

I laughed at the time, and it makes me smile now, but how much did Hannah know about her parents' affairs, her aunts', her grandfather's? Did it normalise infidelity for her? Influence her to embark on the affair that led to her death?

MY GRANDMOTHER EVEN HAD AN AFFAIR, or at least a dalliance, not long after she was married, Susie says. She and my grandfather had gone on holiday with a poet friend and his wife to Yugoslavia, and after a couple of days my grandmother ran off with the poet. My grandfather's 'gloominess' had got to her, she told him when she came back, and he promised to try to be more cheerful.

I had always thought of my grandfather's gloominess as a product of his daughter's suicide. But, reading his diaries, I have learned that it was in him long before Hannah's death. They record periods of gloom, depression, writer's block. 'The long journey home,' he labelled his life during one episode.

In his essay on his childhood, he blamed his father's 'constant amours', which left his mother 'negative and nagging', and affected him in turn. But another source suggests that this gloominess may have been genetic. His parents were friends and colleagues of Chaim Weizmann in the early years of the Zionist movement, and there are dozens of references to them in Weizmann's published letters. These record that my grandfather's mother was a 'terrible Grublergeist', or brooder, even before she met Berthold. And 'Toldy', as Weizmann calls him, though 'a wonderful man and so gifted', was prone to what looks to me suspiciously like depression. 'Toldy is really terribly miserable,' reads a typical letter. He has 'been in bed the whole day and has not said a word'.

Hannah was spared, it seems, the gloomy or Grublergeist genes. By all accounts, her nature was generally cheerful, positive, energetic. Nor, though it is easier to think that suicide is a product of mental illness, is there any evidence that she suffered from depression; there are no stories of her lying in bed all day, and no one has suggested she ever spent a day in silence. But family characteristics we escape genetically can still shape the environment in which we grow up.

When I remember them, in my teens and twenties, my grandparents weren't in conflict with each other. In time, Hannah's death seems to have drawn them together, made them content with less, with each other. I was conscious that a sadness wasn't far beneath the skin in both of them, but they were also funny together, teasing each other, finding humour in their differences. As grandparents, they were warm and generous, their grandparently love vital to both my brother and me. But I can imagine that they weren't always like this as parents.

When my grandfather came home to the cottage on London Road in 1945, after my grandparents had both had 'good wars' apart, my grandmother, Susie says, made him sleep on the sofa, and they never shared a bed again. He was soon working in London, and I imagine that he often stayed in the city overnight.

My grandfather's gloominess and brooding cannot have been a good combination with my grandmother's unreadiness to be pushed beyond her limits. They stayed together, but it is not hard to understand why Hannah was so eager to escape to boarding school. My grandparents were also keen to get away from the family home when they could. When Hannah was fifteen, my grandfather spent several months in America on his Fulbright fellowship; and shortly after he came back, my grandmother went to South Africa, also for a period of months. Hannah was away at boarding school, but it is perhaps not surprising that these parental absences coincided with the period when she had her 'affair' with the headmaster.

I KNOW MYSELF how challenging it can be to have strong-minded teenage girls. My daughters have gone through adolescence in turn as I have been working on Hannah's story, have helped me to understand her, as learning about her has perhaps helped me to understand them. In Hannah's time, teenagers were less well understood. (It is perhaps no coincidence that after Hannah grew up, my grandfather wrote one of the first books about adolescents in Britain — *The Insecure Offenders*, about Teddy Boys.) They weren't allowed to be themselves to the extent they are now, either, though Hannah was never too worried about what was or wasn't allowed, and it is easy to imagine her pushing both her parents beyond their limits.

My grandfather's diaries don't cover this period, but among his papers is a collection of unpublished short stories, including one that is clearly based on Hannah and my grandmother. The girl in the story is called Ann, Hannah's official name. She is fourteen on the day the story is set, the day they are moving house, as Hannah was fourteen when the family moved back into London. The words the story uses to describe Ann — precocious, egotistical, difficult, melodramatic, beautiful — are words used by my grandfather, and others, to describe Hannah.

The story is fiction, rather than memoir, and I don't think my grandmother would ever have been as mean as Lucille is in the story. I can't imagine her calling Hannah a 'blot' on her life, or pulling the trick about the shoes that Lucille does at the end. But I can see her patiently trying to explain to Hannah how her egotism is harming both her and the family.

It is a potent mix — high expectations, as there were from the start with Hannah, and a steady drip of criticism. Did it undermine Hannah's confidence? Leave her, for all her positive nature, vulnerable to failure, rejection?

Stir in, too, her parents' often unhappy relationship, an unhappy household. Did this leave her short of faith in marriage, family life?

Spring 1954 – Autumn 1956

Dear Tash, I am really and truely in love (oh how corny that sounds!) but I really am for the first time in my life — and let me assure you Tash its utter heaven. Pop has given me an open proposal of marriage which I can accept whenever I like and honestly Tash if I feel this way about him this time next year I think I will. I shall be almost nineteen then, and I think if it lasts a year with me it'll be for ever. I really have never felt like this before. The only fly in the ointment is that I'm scared — because he is 23 has had millions of girl friends and while I feel sure that I love him completely now — what will I think in a year?

Last weekend was the happiest time I have ever spent in my life. Pop slept in my bed all night — without either Shirley or Neville knowing. In the evening we went to the Ball. I wish Tash I could convey to you what heaven it was. It was a warm night very clear, the dance was outside, the gardens were all illuminated, Pop danced divinely, it was as tho' we had walked straight out of a woman's own story.

The most blissful moment of the whole weekend was when the landlady in the pub told me not to let my <u>hubby</u> forget to sign the bill!

Dear Tash, By now you must feel as if you have been at Oxford all your life and will always be there. I certainly feel that way about shorthand and secretarial college (vile name) I get progressively worse at typing every day and see my chances of ever getting a job fading very fast. My teacher is a lesbian who bills and coos at us in a mood of flirtatious whimsy (I have absolutely no idea of what I mean by that — probably I feel that I must live up to you in my use of the English language.) Anyway the moral of this sad tale is never be a secretary.

Dear Tash, I am sure Anglo Saxon is pure undiluted heaven compared to the joys of shorthand! I have never found something so diffucult before (you see what it does to my spelling) its completely soulless.

Dear Tash, I do expect an occasional letter — if only to describe to me the life I have somehow managed to miss. I am in bed with flu & Pop is suffering from an attack of sciatica which has rendered him virtually immobile so we have been sitting rather pathetically in our double bed while various doctors mothers & mothers in law bring vast baskets of food and provide pills vile tasting medicines and hot water bottles.

My future as a secretary is I am happy to say becoming less likely every day. I really am quite hopeless at typing. I only wish you were doing it too because as I said before I'm sure you'd be even worse.

Dear Tash, I am thinking very seriously of going to University after all. I think if I do not I shall regret it all my life, and I feel very bad that my academic education ceased at the early age of not quite seventeen. The kind of job I could get at the moment with my limited qualifications that would interest me is very difficult to obtain and the fact that I am married and would have to look at the clock pointedly from 5.30pm onwards would not help matters at all.

Dear Tash, You always refrain from telling me anything but I have heard via the usual grape vine that you have given up M. I do hope you are not too unhappy as I am certain you will find someone much nicer. One of the awful things Frensham has left us with is the feeling that if one is not in love with anyone in particular, life is very dreary, I dont think it need be but it is very hard for me to talk.

190

Nothing very exciting has been happening lately. We are having our doctor and his wife to supper tonight, he is very nice except he looks exactly like one of the seven dwarfs. We went to the opening night of Hamlet with Alan Badel. It was quite terrible Badel is very short and plump and was dressed in ski trousers so that did not improve matters.

Dear Tash, Actually now that I am a fellow stoodent I can view everything from a different angle (my vision is slightly obscured by my college scarf, and my head is aching from my college beret, luckily I am lovely and warm by virtue of my college blazer, and my exquisite black gown.)

The work however is proving fascinating. For the first time I am able to understand what is going on in the world. Our lectures must be very different from those given at Oxford: they seem to be more like classes, and one can interrupt at any time.

Dear Tash, Why do I never see or hear from you? Is it because Pop is a businessman? Or that I don't like Universities and Left Review? Or because I'll only get a fourth?

Twelve

WHAT IS MISSING in all this is a contribution from Hannah herself — her voice, her own words. I have been thinking more and more about her letters to Tasha, and I talk to Susie, and we come up with a plan. We will go to see Tasha together and persuade her to let us look for the letters. But two days before we are due in Oxford, Susie calls. Tasha has had another stroke, and is dead.

A week later, we go instead to Tasha's funeral. Tasha's estranged children do not come, but I meet Esther, her daughter from her second marriage.

It is not the time to ask about the letters, and I store away my thoughts of them. But a couple of months later, Susie mentions she is seeing Sonia, and I ask her to inquire about the letters, and a few days later I receive an email from Esther. She has the letters, but is not sure what to do. There are personal things in them — nothing particularly revealing, but private things about her mother, her aunt.

I understand her hesitation, the draw of secrecy. But now that the letters have been found, I can think of nothing else. I write to Esther, explaining how important they are to me, that my interest is in Hannah, not in Tasha's or Sonia's secrets. She replies that she is going away, and suggests we speak when she returns. The days pass slowly, but eventually she calls to say I can have the letters.

When I arrive at her flat, she has them spread out on the floor. There are about thirty, mostly handwritten, a few typed, on different kinds of paper. I pick one up and try to read it, but I can't concentrate. I am like a man who has never seen a whole book and is let into a library. I am too dizzy to read.

Esther found the letters, she tells me, not hidden away in the attic, but under 'H' in Tasha's filing cabinet. I would have walked past this cabinet when I went to see Tasha.

She wants to make copies of the parts about Tasha and her family, so we go out to a copy shop. When this is done, in the white envelope in which Tasha stored them, Hannah's name circled in black ink on the front, some ten years after I first heard of their existence, I take possession of them. I walk back to the underground station in a daze, and begin reading them on the train. They stretch from when Hannah was fifteen until she was twenty. The loopy handwriting, by now not unfamiliar to me, becomes neater, smaller, as the years pass. The spelling and punctuation and grammar improve a little, though not much.

I am still reading when I reach my station. I get out and sit on a bench while more trains come and go.

IN THE DAYS AFTERWARDS, I do not know what to feel or think. I have dreamed for so long of these letters, what they might tell me, the roads they might open into Hannah's mind. As long as they eluded me, they could be anything. But now that I have them, they are what they are — a teenage girl's letters. They are the nearest to Hannah, the most of her, I will ever get, and it does not seem very much.

I put them on a shelf, and for a couple of weeks I cannot bring myself to look at them again. But eventually I go back to them, read them again more slowly. There might be no great intimations here, nothing beyond the ordinary, but isn't that what I wanted — the

194

ordinary Hannah, the real Hannah?

The Hannah who makes me smile now when I read that 'Sonia only had one line — but she was excellent and showed great signs of talent'; makes me laugh when she writes that 'I dont want to go out much as I have a lot of work to do — lying on the ground breathing in and out'. My mother, I discover, was funny.

I discover, too, that I like her. She could be solipsistic, bossy, dismissive of others, but there is also an openness, a naturalness, in these letters that warms me to her. I have heard about how 'dramatic' she was, her need to be the centre of attention, but while she clearly felt things strongly, said what she thought, she is calmer and softer here than I expected — more wry and self-deprecating than melodramatic ('apart from the fact that I am dead tired and horribly fat life is quite pleasant'.) Her default mode may have been irony and irreverence, which I appreciate, but I am also touched by her youthful earnestness about her acting, the headmaster, my father, university, her advice to Tasha ('you seem in a bad way, but Tash, if he hasn't answered don't for heaven sake write again'.)

It is pleasing to read in her own words about things I have heard from elsewhere, such as secretarial school, which makes more sense now that I see in these letters how young she was, unformed, or RADA, which comes alive to me now for the first time.

There is also disappointment. The fancy-dress party she writes about in one of the letters must have been, from the date, the one where I decided she met my father, but she does not mention him, and he does not appear in the letters for several more months. I reluctantly have to accept that this party was not the occasion when my parents met, or met again.

When she does write about my father, I find her gushing about him, her references to their nights, a little embarrassing. Though that in itself is a new sensation for me — to be getting too much information about my mother, from my mother.

SHE WAS CLEARLY more sexually advanced than the average middle-class girl in the pre-pill era, if that was hardly difficult. Jessica Mann, who was born in the same year as Hannah, writes in *The Fifties Mystique* of conducting a poll among women with whom she had been at Cambridge and finding that the average age of first sexual intercourse was 23.6 years. But the letters suggest Hannah spent more time fending off boys than doing anything with them.

They also seem to confirm what I suspected — that she saw her 'pashes' for boys and her relationship with the headmaster as somehow separate things that could exist alongside each other. 'Look after K,' she writes to Tasha. 'He is much nicer than one imagines in the hols. I had a nice letter from Mike.'

The letters corroborate, in her own words, that something definitely went on with the headmaster. As Shirley had told me, he wrote to her, chased her up to London. He even called in unannounced to her home. Though the letters leave me scarcely the wiser as to what it all meant. He is a 'darling', she writes in one mood. It is comforting to have him 'believing so utterly' in her. She misses him 'like hell'. But when he turns up at the old Frenshamian evening, she 'felt as if I was going to dissolve', and when he tries to get her alone in his Rolls: 'Oh Tash it's upset me ... Godinheaven — its all wrong.'

I search for clues. What does it mean that she uses the word 'affair' to describe what was clearly no more than a flirtation on the airplane to Paris? I look up the Macmurray she writes about as a favourite of the headmaster. John Macmurray was a Scottish philosopher whose central philosophy was that it is in 'community with others that we discover who we really are'. Is this what the headmaster was doing with

Hannah? Being in community with her?

I need help, and I give the letters to a neighbour who is a psychologist and psychoanalyst. Her initial impression, she responds, is 'of a lively and excitable young woman in search of a convincing part for herself in relation to men — femme fatale or vulnerable ingénue, woman of the world or giddy adolescent. It seems impossible from these letters alone to tell whether they actually did or didn't have sexual intercourse because Hannah seems to exaggerate some aspects of what she got up to and to minimise others.'

Though when I tell her about the other evidence I have gathered — Shirley's diary, Bill Will's comments, the headmaster's dismissal, his wife being a schoolgirl and he a teacher when they met — she explains how a young person can be 'inducted' by a powerful older figure. The victim's view of what is right or wrong gets subverted so that she does not realise that 'what is happening is wrong, is taught to talk about abuse as love'.

She talks, and I read up too, about common patterns of abuse. How the person in power tells his victims that they are special, as Hannah wrote of the headmaster idealising her; singles them out for private lessons, as the headmaster invited Hannah to his study for her 'extra German'; inculcates them with his ideas, as he did with Macmurray. It can be difficult, the literature suggests, to distinguish between inspirational teachers and abusive ones: sexual abusers can also be inspirational, which can be specially confusing for the children.

My neighbour explains also about the correlation between sexual abuse and later psychological troubles, including suicide — how these often emerge in the victim's twenties, the childhood experiences leaving the victim 'brittle'. The fact that Hannah was a strong personality wouldn't necessarily have helped, she says; 'the whole of that terrific force gets turned against herself'.

197

IS THAT HOW it was with Hannah? Her letters don't say, don't reveal any such darkness, take me only anyway to the age of twenty. This is all I have of her voice, that 'husky voice', as my grandfather wrote in his diary. With its 'slight South African accent', Hannah wrote to Tasha. 'Such a pleasant, well-modulated voice,' Phyll Willmott wrote in her diary. 'A singularly expressive part of her whole personality. She could "pun" with it when pleased, chuckle with it or grin when amused, and use it as a hammer when arguing fiercely about this or that.'

But there are still a few other voices to hear — including the two witnesses to her last months, last days, who my grandfather sought out after her death. I can no more speak to Anne Wicks than I can Hannah, but after reading Hannah's letters it occurs to me that Anne might have left letters or diaries that could throw light on Hannah's story. An obituary mentions a close friend in the advertising world. I call her, and she offers to pass on a message to Anne's children.

While I am waiting, I go through the entries about Anne in my grandfather's diaries. After his talk with her, he wrote that she was 'not as much a villain' as my father suggested; but as time passes, his references grow more critical again. At first, he writes only that she was a 'hypnotic influence', but in April 1966, four months after Hannah's death, he says something more specific: Anne told Hannah that publishing *The Captive Wife* would do 'irreparable harm' to her career. In December 1967, the second anniversary of Hannah's death, he expands this to Anne having 'depressed Hannah about her book, her marriage, her prospects'. And in 1969 he elaborates a little further: 'Anne Wicks saying a) leave your husband b) John'll never marry you c) your work is preposterous.'

Armed with these allegations, I go back to my father. He was angry with Anne, he says, because she 'encouraged' Hannah to have an affair. Anne had left her husband, 'was enjoying her newfound freedom,

198

and made Hannah feel that she was missing out on life'. But Anne's marriage to Tony wasn't 'serious' like his and Hannah's; it only lasted a few years, and there weren't any children.

He doesn't know anything about Anne telling Hannah that John Hayes would never marry her, though she was right. He did know that Anne was 'very down on' *The Captive Wife*, and that 'Hannah took these criticisms very seriously'. She told Hannah it would 'ruin her reputation', though he can't say why.

To my surprise, he says that Anne wrote to him not long before she died, asking to meet him. What did he do? I ask. Tore up the letter and threw it away, he says. Did he think she was writing because she knew she had cancer? He didn't know, he says, didn't want to meet. What good would it have done?

I AM ONLY MORE INTRIGUED, though. What kind of friend was Anne Wicks? What kind of person? Are my father's, my grandfather's, accusations justified?

My grandfather kept only two of the transcripts of his interviews for his book about intellectuals: Hannah's and Anne Wicks's. Hannah, I presume, recommended Anne to my grandfather.

'From Bromley, Kent,' he noted. 'Father, bricklayer. 11-plus. Went to Bromley Grammar School. Why not try for Oxbridge? It seemed out of reach.'

Like Hannah, she started a PhD in sociology at Bedford 'but gave it up. Felt that working in too much isolation.'

Instead Hannah gave her an introduction to my grandfather's friend Mark Abrams, whose name had helped Hannah get into Bedford. Anne got 'a good basic training' in social and market research at Abrams's company, and went to work at Thomson newspapers, where she was made head of market research at the age of twenty-six.

'I don't take any notice of the fact that I'm a woman,' she said, 'and I don't let anyone else do so.' She no longer had 'much contact with girls at Bedford College but knows that a high proportion of them have a husband and two children and have stopped working entirely'. Single again herself, she said that when women marry, they seem to her to 'turn into cabbages overnight'.

INSTEAD OF ANNE'S CHILDREN, I hear from Di Hibel, a friend of Anne's they ask to contact me. Di was at Bedford, too, she tells me when we meet, though a couple of years behind Hannah and Anne. She remembers seeing Hannah once in the library. She was pregnant with me, and wearing a man's shirt.

'Annie,' as she calls her, as Hannah had on her suicide note, 'was very angry with Hannah for what she did to her,' Di says. 'She told me she did it in her flat, and she didn't want to talk about it.'

Anne never married — 'was wedded to her job' — though she had three children by two different fathers, Di says. She had a successful career in market research and account planning. She became a Thatcherite in her later years, and even considered trying to become a Tory MP.

DI DOESN'T KNOW ABOUT — Anne's children didn't mention — any diaries or letters, but instead serendipity opens another door. Tony Wicks had talked of some friends of Anne, a couple who lived in Chalcot Square, but I have almost forgotten about them until I hear my sister-in-law mentioning their uncommon name. Margaret and Rainer Schuelein, it turns out, are her next-door neighbours — were my brother's neighbours for the last fifteen years of his life.

I have often seen them, I realise, have even said hello to them on the street. Now I call them, and they invite me round. They are gentle, soft spoken. 'Annie,' they say, was 'the most wonderful friend.' She was 'charming, bright, opinionated, full of life'.

They knew Hannah a bit — they had dinner with her and my father and Anne and Tony a couple of times. They moved to this house before Hannah died, and Margaret even remembers Hannah coming here once. She doesn't think she came in, but can remember her standing on the front drive with Anne. She was with her son in a pushchair — with me, it must have been.

I ask if they ever said anything to Simon. No, they say, they weren't sure he would have wanted them to tell him. 'Once something is said it can't be unsaid,' they say. It might have created unease between neighbours.

Were they still friends with Anne when my brother was living next door? I ask. 'Oh, yes,' they say. 'Annie often came here.'

I try to imagine her sitting in this room while my brother was a few feet away on the other side of the dividing wall. Perhaps she sat on sunny days in the garden while my brother and his boys were playing on their grass. Did the boys ever kick a ball across, did she pick it up, hand it back to her friend's son, one of her friend's grandsons? Perhaps it was after such a moment that she wrote to my father, asking to meet him. I ask the Schueleins, but they can't say, didn't know that Anne had written to my father, though she knew who their neighbour was.

They show me some photographs of a young Anne — a tall, large-boned, good-looking young woman, her short dress emphasising a belly swollen in pregnancy, her hair in a similar Mary Quant bob to Hannah's.

They have something else to show me, too: Margaret's diary from 1965. Anne and her boyfriend, it reveals, had supper with them the night Hannah died. She shows me the page: 'Supper Ghriam and Annie and pheasant here.'

I stare at these words, try to make sense of them. Of course, once she had told my grandparents, Anne wouldn't have wanted to go back to her flat, would have sought out her boyfriend, her friends, for company and solace. I understand that Margaret might not have wanted to write about Hannah's suicide in her diary. But there is something about the 'pheasant' that upsets me — that this was what she chose to note in her diary on the day of Hannah's suicide in Anne's flat, that she and Anne and their men supped on pheasant.

I COMPOSE MYSELF, can hardly blame acquaintances for the evasions that my own family were guilty of, that I have been guilty of. And there are questions I still need to ask, about my father's and grandfather's allegations.

It was true, they say, when I ask about Anne encouraging Hannah to have an affair, that Anne thought my father too 'manly and controlling', though the way they saw it, the two women 'egged each other on to reject their husbands'.

They agree, though, that Anne was 'negative' about Hannah's book. 'She thought Hannah had based it on too small a group of people, too small to be serious.' As they say this, I think I understand. *The Captive Wife* was a work of qualitative research, based on conversations with ninety-six women. Anne, in contrast, was a quantitative market researcher, used to polling thousands of people. To her, Hannah's book would have been statistically meaningless.

Though it is only later that the irony sinks that it was Hannah who introduced Anne to Mark Abrams, who trained her in statistical research.

AS I AM LEAVING, I mention my hopes about Anne's papers, thinking that the Schueleins might put in a good word with her children, but

Margaret tells me instead that she has some letters from Anne — from the period just after Hannah died. They went abroad for a year, and Anne house-sat for them and looked after their affairs, dealt with their post, 'forged our signatures on everything'.

She'll have to find the letters, Margaret says, and the next day she calls, and I go back and read them on a table against the party wall with my brother's house.

The top one is dated 14 January 1966, exactly a month after Hannah's death. Anne writes of being invited to supper with Hannah's Hornsey colleague, Michael Kidron, and his wife, Nina. 'It was a rather nice evening, slightly saddened for me because Nina had only the day before heard of Hannah's death and was anxious to know why it could have happened. I filled in some of the background for her because she knew the basis of the story anyway.'

Anne feels 'a bit bad about having broken a sort of promise' to my father, presumably not to talk about Hannah's death, 'but the story Nina had was worse for him in that she thought he had left her'. She put off seeing some other people, she writes, 'because I don't want to go through the Hannah saga again'.

'Incidentally,' she writes, 'isn't it a small world?':

Wicks knows Schueleins
Schueleins know Kidrons
Wicks knows Gavrons
Gavrons knows Kidrons.

In the next letter, a month or so later, she writes of deciding to stay on in her flat rather than buy a place, 'because it is just too complicated and I thought it would be nice to have a bit of spare cash for a while rather than taking on another heavy financial commitment now'. She has had 'a bad patch' when she 'replaced my Hannah miseries' with miseries about the two men she is seeing, but is better now. She ends by sending her affections to the Schueleins' son, Max. 'I am terribly sorry to miss several months of Max growing up.'

I understand, as with Margaret's diary, that these letters do not tell the whole story, that what we say and what we feel are seldom the same thing. But I still can't help being taken aback by some of the things she writes, her tone, what she does not write. The 'Hannah saga', for example, as if the main thing about Hannah's death was that it was irksome to her. The dance of people who know each other that doesn't mention that one of these people has stopped dancing. When she writes of her sadness at missing months of her friend's son's life, I wonder whether it occurred to her that Hannah would be missing all of her own sons' lives — that we would be missing all of Hannah's.

The last letter is dated 14 December, the date of Hannah's death, and at first I assume it is a year later, but as I read it I realise that it is from a year earlier. Anne has been to the ballet with Hannah, and 'absolutely loved it'. She has also 'found a flat — in Chalcot Square. There was a board up so I phoned the agent, and then I went to see it this morning.' It is the flat where Hannah died, and I read her description of its rooms — the kitchen 'smaller than yours but larger than mine and quite large enough to eat in comfortably'.

I HAVE HAD John Hayes's telephone number for a year now, without finding the courage to call him. A friend of my stepmother knows him. He still lives, she told me, with the man he was living with when he was seeing Hannah, who is also called John. The two Johns, she calls them.

Not for the first time, I sit with the number and a phone in front of me. Even this makes me nervous. This is the man who had an affair with my mother, 'cuckolded' my father. Over whom she killed herself.

It is mid-morning. He is probably out, I tell myself. What if I just dial, listen to his voice on the answer machine?

I watch my finger move from one key to the next, listen to the echo of the rings. One, two. Before I can hang up, a man's voice answers, says that he is John.

I panic. Which John is it? I am looking for John Hayes, I say.

'This is John Hayes.'

The voice is softer, posher, more velvety than I have imagined — though what I have imagined I do not know, only not this, perhaps not anything.

I could still hang up, but I do not. I explain, as well as I can, my hand shaking, who I am, what I want, and the velvety voice responds slowly, calmly. Yes, he will see me, he says. He is going to the physio for his neck tomorrow, and it always hurts for several days afterwards, so he suggests we meet one day next week, at the Charing Cross Hotel, in the upstairs café.

An hour later, he calls back. There is a tremor in his voice now. He has been disturbed by my phone call, he says. We should meet sooner. Tomorrow. He will come into town after his physio. The same place.

I hardly sleep. I arrive early at the hotel and I go upstairs, but there is a function in the café, so it is closed to the general public. I come down to the lobby and walk up and down until I realise that I have twice, three times, walked past a man hunched in a scarf and coat in a chair in an alcove.

I look at him. He looks at me. John? Yes.

He stands up; we shake hands. He is smaller than I imagined — in my mind he has always been tall. He is older, too — I was looking, I realise, for a younger man. Though he is no older than his age. White

205

hair, a squarish face, watery blue eyes. In an email later, he will tell me that he, too, hardly slept the previous night.

We sit. Perhaps we discuss drinks, order them. I do not remember. I explain again my need to know about Hannah. He will answer any questions, he says, though when I ask if I can take notes he looks alarmed. Better not, he says. His voice seems less velvety in person, more pained, kindlier.

I suggest we start at the beginning, his first meeting with Hannah, and he says it was 1964 — no, 65. 'What year was it?' he says, fumbling over his words.

I help him work out the date, my journalist self taking control. It was the autumn of 1964 — he arrived at the college a year after Hannah.

What was his impression of Hannah? I ask.

'She was the princess of the college,' he says.

'I have to write that down,' I say, and he says okay, and from here on I take notes.

What does he mean by princess? I ask.

'One she was beautiful, and two she had an intense clarity of mind that burned like the sun,' he says. 'By princess, I mean she was the person in control — she quickly established herself as the leading member of our group, and put others in the shade.'

He is more confident now, and he talks with a quiet, staccato eloquence about Hornsey, how the general studies course was new, how he and Hannah and others were forging it together, would have discussions, arguments. He and Hannah were 'quite antagonistic to each other at first, belligerent even'. He was a grammar-school boy who had been to Oxford to study philosophy, he says, so he was 'quite confident himself, quite bright and brash'.

'Hannah and I were the children, twenty-eight, twenty-nine,

the youngest in the department,' he says. 'The belligerence grew into affection.'

I have to understand the times, he says. 'There was an effervescence in the air. A feeling that we could do things, Britain itself seemed at that moment capable of creating a dynamic new culture, cinema, theatre. Hannah and I were drunk on this metaphorically, and it created an alliance between us.'

It was an uneasy alliance at first. 'Hannah used to drop in halfway through my lectures and sit at the back and make herself conspicuous, as was her style. The first time this happened I said, "What are you doing snooping on my lecture," and she said, "I want to see what you're like. You're new, are you any good?"'

He remembers one occasion. 'We were interviewing candidates, students, and she said I should start, so I asked this schoolboy whether he thought flowers could feel pain. I wanted to ask him something he wouldn't be prepared for. And Hannah snorted. I ignored her, asked my questions, and she asked hers, but at the break I asked her why she had been so ill-mannered, and she said I was being so Oxford and pompous.' They laughed; the ice was broken.

He and the other John met at Oxford and had been together for ten years by the time he met Hannah. They had both had affairs, but he had never slept with a woman before Hannah, and has never done so since. So why her? I ask. 'I was intoxicated by her combination of beauty and clarity and candour.'

He had 'always been attracted intellectually, emotionally, to women'. But with Hannah there was a 'physical intensity', a passion, that intrigued him.

Hannah made the running, set up their meetings in Anne Wicks's flat, though they only met there three or four times in total. He wasn't very good with her in bed; she had to encourage him, as he found it a bit tawdry. 'That step to me was a step I shouldn't have taken,' he says. Before the summer, the relationship had been 'all about affection, a hidden affection, which produces an intensity in itself'. It was only after the summer that it became sexual.

What he cared about was the 'wonderful mutuality' they had with each other, the excited intellectual talk. 'We were in a highly combustible state in our excitement over ideas. We had the feeling that what we talked about mattered.'

But once they had taken the step into bed, Hannah started getting more serious. He didn't know that my father had moved out and, when he did, John was 'disturbed morally'. He came 'from a small rural community in Lancashire and had a very ethical system of living'. He was pulled along by Hannah, but 'after a time I felt I didn't want to go any further, and I began to pull back'.

A couple of Saturdays before Hannah died, she hosted a party at our house for staff and students from Hornsey. My father was there, too. 'It was the first time I met your father, or at least saw him. I don't think we actually met. But I looked across a room and knew who he was, and I was sure that he knew who I was.'

This was 'crucial' for John — coming to our house, seeing my father, seeing my brother's and my toothbrushes in the bathroom. 'I saw her family, and realised I was committing adultery.' He got 'very drunk, and went into the bathroom and covered the mirror with messages in shaving foam'.

There was another episode the week before Hannah died. He went out for lunch with her, and she said she wanted to show him something, 'and we walked along a street and she pointed up at a flat and said, "That's where we are going to live," and I said, "We?" and she said, "Yes, you and I! We can make a go of it. I'll have the children with me, of course."'

John had a 'major recoil'. He suddenly realised she was being serious, that this was more than an adventure for her.

They had arranged to meet on the afternoon of Hannah's death at Anne Wicks's flat, but he rang her the night before or that morning to say he wasn't coming, that they had to stop. 'We argued, and she said, "I'll still be there if you change your mind."'

He had a six o'clock lecture, but afterwards he decided he 'wasn't dealing with this in the proper manner' and that he needed to talk to her face to face. 'I went to Chalk Farm station, and when I got out I thought I'd ring the flat to see if she was there, but I got no reply. I called her home, and your father answered and said she was dead.'

Anne Wicks had told my grandfather that she had found John on her steps. This might be true, he says, but he has no memory of it. He knows that he eventually went home that night. The other John knew about Hannah, so he was able to tell him what had happened, but they never talked about it. I ask why. 'You carry on with life.'

He has often thought about it, though. 'In trying to come to terms with it,' he says, 'I came to believe that she'd embarked on something and it hadn't worked.' He believes the act itself was 'spur of the moment', but thinks 'it was in her mind as an abstract idea for some time', and that when her fantasy of making a new life with him was 'pricked', she 'went for it'.

'I think of my own stupidity, carelessness,' he says, shaking his head sadly.

Of Hannah's personality he says, 'Aut Caesar aut nihil' — either Caesar or nothing.

'She wanted clarity,' he says. 'She couldn't live with imperfection, compromise.' Later, typing up my notes, I think about this: how we have all had to live with the compromises she left for us.

His meeting with my grandfather was 'civilised', he says. He was still in a state of shock, feeling completely negative about himself, but my grandfather gave him 'a rope to pick myself up a bit' — 'a picture of someone who was in psychological turmoil'.

He asked for a piece of her jewelry, but my grandfather told him that was 'impossible'.

I ask about the sleeping pills he told my grandfather that she carried, but he doesn't remember saying that — or about any pills.

He saw my father once more, on an early-morning flight from Venice. 'I recognised him, he was with his new wife, we exchanged glances — nothing more.'

He has had close women friends since Hannah, though never quite like Hannah, and never anything sexual. He mentions the novelist Angela Carter, and the publisher Carmen Callil, an old friend of my father's.

Did he ever talk to Carmen about Hannah?

This is the first time he has ever spoken of her, he says.

We have both spent much of the conversation in tears, and his cheeks are wet now. 'She is always there in my mind,' he says. 'The ghost comes back.'

From *The Captive Wife*, 1966

This is a study about women, and in particular about young women.

With the industrial revolution men followed work from the home to the factory and women became dependent on men, not only in economic terms but also in terms of a whole pattern of psychological subtleties within their relationships.

What constituted the essential 'femaleness' of the female revealed how deeply ideas of her inferiority were taken as part of the natural order of things.

The concept of romantic love drawing its inspiration largely from legends about knights and ladies is still with us.

The ambivalence in our society towards sexual behaviour, with a widening degree of permissiveness in private, while in public the Victorian attitudes remain.

In 1960 more than one quarter of all brides were under twenty.

'I must have been mad,' said one. 'I didn't have a clue.'

'I was too young. But I had no choice. I wanted desperately to get away from my parents and this seemed the right way to do it.'

The nature of the role of a girl in the family is such as to make her more exposed to family disturbances than that of the boy.

Nothing has prepared young wives for the relentless boredom of scrubbing floors and ironing shirts.

'My husband simply doesn't believe in doing housework.'

The birth of the first child, however, caused a much greater change than had marriage.

It changed them from being a new kind of woman to being the traditional woman.

'Of course I must be with them all the time,' said a teacher's wife, 'though I must confess that sometimes I *long* to get away.'

Only recently has the married woman attempted to combine home and work simultaneously.

They want to work, and feel curiously functionless when not working, but at the same time they sense their great responsibilities towards the children.

Constant pressure on girls to play down and discipline an ambition that society at the same time continually stimulates.

An air of confusion which hangs over the whole question of women and their position in society.

Over what precisely constitutes the psychology of the female.

The situation at present is one of conflict and stress.

Thirteen

I DON'T REMEMBER when I first discovered the copies of *The Captive Wife* on their high shelf in our house, but for a time in my teenage years, when I knew I would not be disturbed, I would climb on to the back of the sofa beneath and pull them out. There was the Pelican paperback, with its cover photograph of a woman and two young children who for some reason weren't my mother, my brother, and me; the delicate Japanese edition, with its rice-paper dust sleeve and columns of hieroglyphics; and the official-looking Routledge & Kegan Paul hardback, with its chalk-blue cover and wad of newspaper cuttings tucked inside.

I never made any attempt to read the book, but I liked to read the acknowledgements at the front: to my grandfather, my father, and our nanny, 'for her help in sharing the care of my children'. I didn't read the cuttings properly, either, but looking through them for Hannah's name, and the references to 'an outstanding young talent' or 'a life tragically cut short', gave me a strangely pleasurable knot in my stomach.

When I was at university, a new edition of *The Captive Wife* was published, with an introduction by the sociologist and novelist Ann Oakley. I didn't know it was being reissued until Susie gave me a copy. It was the first copy of my mother's book I had owned; the first I had held in my hand that I hadn't taken surreptitiously from a high shelf.

I still didn't read it, but I looked at the introduction. I had met Ann Oakley once at Susie's house — she and Susie were friends from university — and Susie had said something then about Ann being fascinated by Hannah, which made me suspicious of her. But I was still shocked to find her revealing in her opening sentence that Hannah had killed herself.

I know now that this was widely known, that some of my own boyhood friends even knew, but at the time I still believed it was a close family secret. I had spoken about it only once myself since my father had told me, blurting it out in an argument with a girlfriend, and afterwards feeling ashamed of myself, and I saw Ann Oakley's act as a betrayal of my family.

I didn't like, either, the familiarity she claimed with Hannah, writing that her life had 'touched' Hannah's because she was friends with Susie and had followed Hannah to the Bedford sociology department, writing a doctorate, which also became a book, on housework.

I didn't like the way she tried to appropriate Hannah's book, as I saw it, for her own feminist cause: 'the problematic of women's own needs'.

And I especially didn't like her writing that Hannah's death 'could hardly have been unrelated to the dilemmas and contradictions of women's situation'. I was twenty-one, still working out what it meant to be a man, and I felt she was insinuating something here about men, about the men in my family, perhaps even about me — though exactly what, I don't think I could have said.

I TOOK THE BOOK with me on my travels, put it on my shelves in each new place I lived, but I still didn't read it. I didn't read it either when I came back to England and found Hannah's suicide note and the report

216

of her inquest. Even after Simon died, and all those feelings welled up in me, I didn't read it. When I wrote my article about Hannah in the *Guardian*, I still hadn't read it.

It was partly, I think, that I was afraid I wouldn't find it interesting. It was the only significant piece of my mother I had, and I didn't want to ask too many questions of it and find out it was just another old book. Though I was also perhaps wary, even before I read Ann Oakley's introduction, of the accusation I saw myself in the title — the suggestion that this was a book critical of men. I had already been rejected once by my mother. Did I want to read the only piece of her she had left and find myself, as a man, rejected again?

EARLY IN THE SUMMER after my newspaper article came out, I went round to my old house to claim the copies of her book and the cuttings inside the hardback. I suppose I must have noticed before that there were other books on sociological and connected matters on the shelves, but it was only now that I properly took in that these must have been Hannah's. Standing again on the back of the sofa — a newer sofa, but in the same position — I looked through them.

Most had probably not been opened since Hannah last did so. Inside one, held in place by a rusty paper clip, I found a letter from the books editor of the *Economist*, from 31 May 1965, asking for a review of 500–600 words. In another, I found the handwritten draft of a book review.

Many of the books had Hannah's signature in the front, the writing growing less loopy with age. In the front of one was a different signature, in a spiky hand — J. F. Hayes. I hadn't yet spoken to my stepmother's friend who knew John Hayes, and Susie had told me she thought his name was Haynes, but I knew who this was. I stared at the signature, wondering that the book had moved house with us, had sat here all through my childhood, through the years my father had lived here. I am not sure until that moment that I properly understood that this man, the homosexual lover in my father's story, was a real person.

In some, Hannah had underlined passages or made marks in the margins, as I do when I am reading — as my father, who was a printer, is a bibliophile, would never do. In one, there was even a squiggle where her pen must have run dry and she had pressed the nib into the paper to make the ink flow again.

Each time I came across one of these marked passages, I would read it for clues to her mind. Was there something significant in her interest in puberty rites among the Apache? In the feelings of isolation of prison officers? In the lost comfort and security of Bruno Bettelheim's Viennese youth?

Halfway along a shelf, I came to a book with the same chalk-blue cover as the hardback of her book — Emile Durkheim's classic of 1897 *Suicide: a study in sociology*, published in the same Routledge & Kegan Paul series as *The Captive Wife* would be a few years later.

Turning the pages, I saw pen marks, and I sat down on the sofa to read:

No living being can be happy or even exist unless his needs are sufficiently proportioned to his means.

A man of low morality will kill another rather than himself.

Every individual has what we may call a suicide-potential, a tendency to self-murder.

Even if it were proved that the average man never kills himself and that only those do so who show certain anomalies, this would still not justify considering insanity a necessary condition of suicide.

What was Hannah thinking when she read these passages? The edition was published in 1963, and she might have read it any time between then and her death. Was she already having suicidal thoughts when she did so? Or did reading this book help to put the idea into her mind?

Between the final pages of the text, I found something else: the desiccated remains of a tiny flower. It is still there in the book. The sap has long been absorbed by the paper, leaving ghostly brown impressions on either page, making the flower hard to identify. But it looks to me as if it was once a daisy, picked, I guess, from our garden and put here — though by whom, and why, I do not know.

LATER THAT SUMMER, as my Hannah researches progressed, I finally made myself, or perhaps allowed myself to, read *The Captive Wife*. I was pleasantly surprised by how fluently it was written, with the commas in all the right places. The opening section, a survey of women's position in society and the family since Victorian times, was impressively informative, interesting. But the main part, in which the results of her interviews were laid out, I found harder work.

I read, as Hannah would have, with a pen in my mind, though I didn't find much to mark. I put a line beside a section on teenage brides, and underlined the comments of a 'company director's wife', as Hannah had been, who had married at eighteen and regretted that she hadn't gone to university. 'I sometimes feel as if my brain is disintegrating,' Hannah quoted her as saying. Though, beside this, I wrote 'Hannah?' Her brain hadn't been disintegrating — she had gone to university, got a degree, a doctorate, written this book.

I was even disappointed, for all my worries that it would be anti-man, at how mild it was. The newspapers, with their 'So lonely in the real Coronation Street' headlines, had focused on its most dramatic findings. But most of the text was taken up with more workmanlike sections on childhood, marriage, housework, friendship, leisure, work. The grist of the book was as much about class as gender, that things were harder for working-class women, who didn't have gardens, couldn't afford childcare, were less qualified to return to work later.

In its conclusion, it didn't even argue for equality with men — only for better childcare facilities, more part-time employment, education that would better prepare women for their 'multiplicity' of roles.

Most disappointing was how little of Hannah there seemed to be in these pages. The book was a work of academic sociology, containing nothing, it seemed to me, of her own voice, of her own feelings, thoughts, personality.

IT WAS PARTLY, I can see now, that I knew so little about Hannah and her world, partly the fears and prejudices I still held to, my reluctance to accept that Hannah might have been a captive wife in any way. It is a measure, then, of what I have learned in the intervening years, both about Hannah and her world, and about myself, that when I read the book now I find more of her in it, more of her own conflicts.

When I read it now, for example, I think that it wasn't a coincidence that the average age of her mothers was twenty-six, as she was when she began interviewing them, and that the average number of children they had was two.

When I read now about the 'relentless boredom of scrubbing floors and ironing shirts', I think about the early months of her marriage when she was learning to be a housewife; how Jeanie told me Hannah always had supper on the table for my father; always used one cloth for wiping surfaces and another for dishes.

When I read that the 'major psychological turning point' for young women was not marriage but the first child, I think of Hannah's own psyche as a young mother, her trouble bonding with Simon when she had him at twenty-one. When she writes that every one of her interviewees felt 'compelled to stay at home with their children', whatever 'their own personal desires', I think of her breezy statement to an *Evening Standard* journalist that she didn't mind 'Simon thinking he has two mothers', and wonder whether this was what she really felt. Whether the story of the baby with two heads was a truer window into her own thoughts and feelings.

When she writes of Victorian ideas of 'female inferiority', and how in 'the work situation' in her own time 'many of the attitudes to women are based firmly on past ideologies', I think of her experiences in the academic world, her struggle to get the subject of her thesis approved, the delay in the awarding of her doctorate, her rejection by the LSE as a 'lightweight'.

BUT IF I can now see that there is more of Hannah in *The Captive Wife* than I had found before, the book is still, as Ann Oakley wrote in the introduction, 'tantalising in what it does not say, in what it is not able to tell us about its own conception, gestation and birth, and about the regard in which its author held it and herself'.

At twenty-one, I resented Ann's claims of familiarity with Hannah, but now I go to see her in search of her impressions of Hannah and the times they lived in.

She is only a few years younger than Hannah would have been, but she seems ageless, the fire still in her. When she agreed to write the introduction, she tells me, she decided she needed to find out more about Hannah's death, so she went to see my grandparents and my father. They were 'welcoming, not hostile or difficult', but she felt that she could go only 'so far and no further' — that even seventeen years after Hannah's death, there were questions they weren't willing to answer.

My grandfather did show her Hannah's suicide note. She was 'shocked' that he hadn't shown it to my brother or me, and tried to persuade him to do so, though it remained among his papers, where I found it.

In her introduction, she wrote that the timing of *The Captive Wife*, several years before the second wave of the women's movement, made it 'more remarkable' but also 'more limited'. It was a 'wonderful title', she says now, 'but a more pedestrian study'. She has always wondered how much Hannah was held back by her supervisors, by what they said, or what she worried they might say. She was pushing the boundaries with her choice of subject, and perhaps she felt she had to demonstrate more than the usual academic objectivity.

I have to remember, Ann says, how difficult it was for a woman academic in the 1960s, and particularly for a woman academic writing about the situation of women. When Ann registered to start her own PhD at Bedford in 1969, 'the senior academics were all men, and none were sympathetic to the idea of housework as a valid subject for study'. ('The man I finally ended up with as my supervisor tended to think at first that what I was talking about was the harmony or disharmony of the marital bed,' she has written, 'or, at the very least, the marvellous things that could be done with the handles of vacuum cleaners.')

Ann was fortunate that the first women's groups were starting. There was one at Bedford, where she was able to air her frustrations and receive moral support, but even so her supervisor often had her in tears. For Hannah, starting her thesis a decade earlier, it must have been 'much more difficult'. She would have been 'very alone academically —

there simply weren't other women to talk to doing similar subjects, and the male academics could make life very difficult'.

THERE ARE TWO particular male academics I want to ask Anne about, but I am nervous about the first one — Richard Titmuss, the LSE professor who supposedly made the comment about Hannah wearing too much eye make-up — as he was Ann's father. But when I tell her the story, she says, 'Oh, yes, that sounds like my father.' She has even heard the story before, though about a different young woman — and I wonder aloud whether perhaps the story wasn't about Hannah. As far as I know, and as photographs suggest, too, Hannah hardly ever wore make-up.

'If it wasn't eye make-up, it would have been something else,' Ann says with a shrug. Her father was in theory a great advocate of social justice, she says, but he 'didn't like women, and he especially didn't like working women' — he could be 'vitriolic' to them, and didn't like having them around the LSE. She can easily imagine that he would have found an excuse not to hire Hannah.

The other man I ask about is O. R. McGregor, Hannah's lecturer and later professor at Bedford — the 'enemy', as my grandfather called him in his diary when Hannah was rejected by the LSE. After Hannah's death, my grandfather wrote of seeing an article McGregor had written about equality for women, and wanting to 'write and accuse him'.

I asked my father, but all he could remember was that McGregor in some way delayed her thesis and blocked her academic path. McGregor 'must have felt guilty', he said, because after Hannah's death my father got into a train carriage with McGregor, who 'scuttled away' when they saw each other.

Ann got on well with McGregor herself, she says. When she had her problems with her supervisor, McGregor was supportive to her. He wasn't specifically anti-women like her father, but 'if he didn't like you, he could give you a very hard time'. He was a 'difficult man, a great manipulator'.

SHE SUGGESTS I get in touch with another former LSE professor of sociology, Terrence Morris, who was the same generation as Hannah. I send him an email, and he writes back immediately: 'I may be able to help you with my recollections of the LSE of nearly fifty years ago, not least since Oliver McGregor and Richard Titmuss were people whom I knew well. Each was different but equally puissant. No-one with any sense of self-preservation would have wished to cross them.'

He never met Hannah, but he knew about her and he recalled 'the suspicion that she had not been fairly treated in respect of her applications to the LSE. Times were not easy for young academics, not least since many professors approached human relations in their departments in a fashion that owed something to the culture of patronage in the Middle Ages. It was specially tough for women.'

Things were beginning to change in the early 1960s, he tells me, when I go to see him. But the elite was still an 'old guard of academics, many of whom had been civil servants in the war, and imported into academia a patrician civil-service attitude'. McGregor produced 'a lot of misery', he says. 'He was a schemer. I can say from personal experience that he would tell you one thing and do another, depending on what suited him.' He could be 'very spiteful'.

He doesn't know any specific details about Hannah. There was 'lots of smoke, but he doesn't have the gun', though the pattern was repeated with other women. He talks of Eileen Younghusband, a distinguished expert on social work, who was 'pushed out of the LSE by Titmuss', and Nancy Seear, who was 'also treated badly'. The joke was 'what's that

224

scrabbling noise — it's [a particular woman] trying to get promoted'.

HE SUGGESTS A WOMAN SOCIOLOGIST, Bernice Martin, who might be able to tell me more. He offers to email her on my behalf, and later forwards her reply. Bernice, it turns out, was at Bedford with Hannah, considered her a friend, and also taught there later with McGregor. She knew, she writes, that there were 'issues' between 'Mac' and Hannah:

Mac called me into his office on the day he heard about her death to ask me for reassurance that his lukewarm references, which he knew had stopped her getting a job at the LSE, couldn't have been the cause of her suicide. I couldn't reassure him because I had no idea what had happened in her life. He excused himself by saying she was more a clever journalist than a real scholar, and that Hornsey was the right place for her, but I sensed that this was an excuse to save his conscience rather than a real conviction.

'I have only good memories of Hannah,' she concludes:

She was everything I was not — cosmopolitan, cultured, effortlessly charming while I was a single-minded working-class scholarship girl painfully learning about the big world. But we admired and liked each other though our worlds barely touched. Jeremy ought to know what a very lovely young woman his mother was and what a tragedy and waste so many people thought her death.

I write back, and we meet at Clapham Junction station and head out onto the street to find a café. Walking beside her, I feel happy. It

225

is partly that she wrote so enthusiastically about Hannah, talks now about her with such warmth, though I have felt this happiness meeting others of Hannah's female friends. Am I, in my search for my mother, taking any motherliness I can get along the way?

Bernice didn't see Hannah much after she left Bedford, she says, but a year or so before Hannah died — around the time she was rejected by the LSE — she bumped into her in Baker Street, and Hannah said to her then, 'You don't think that Mac would give me a bad reference on purpose?' She can't remember what she told Hannah then, but she says now that she can 'absolutely believe' that McGregor would have sabotaged Hannah's application to the LSE.

I ask if it might have been a clash of wills — two strong characters. But she says it was more complicated, more insidious, than that. 'Academia was an elite, an empire.' McGregor 'liked controlling the job market in sociology in London, and he was a man who preferred people who were beholden to him', and Hannah's work and character undermined and challenged his position.

It was partly Hannah's qualitative approach, which older sociologists like McGregor were suspicious of. It was partly, too, that while he was publicly pro women, he was 'uncomfortable with the first stirrings of feminist assertiveness that Hannah represented, which otherwise politically leftist men of his generation were inclined to sneer at as the whingeing of privileged young women'.

Most importantly perhaps, McGregor wanted to influence public ideas and government legislation, 'to be like Sidney and Beatrice Webb'. Although his magnum opus was a work on divorce, his position on the contemporary family was that it was 'healthy and happy for the most part', whereas Hannah's work revealed a more constricting pattern of family life for women.

Hannah's work was 'perhaps only a minor political embarrassment' for McGregor, but that would have been enough for him to want to deny her 'the sort of prominence that could undermine his optimistic predictions about the stable family just at the point when his influence was rising'.

Of course, Bernice says, Hannah may well have 'got up Mac's nose personally'. She remembers a cabaret at the Bedford sociology graduation party of 1959 at which Hannah had organised a skit about McGregor and another teacher based on a Calypso song. Nothing like that had been done before at Bedford, she says, and she doesn't imagine McGregor liked it very much.

'He wasn't used to people who stood up to him and did something different. Hannah was moving in a new direction, she was a pioneer, what she was doing was quite new in England, and she was doing it herself, from within herself.'

'The sense she gave to people like me was that there was more to life than you'd seen and she was determined to have it,' she says. 'But she was struggling against strong men. Even strong women buckled under that sort of pressure.'

THE GENERAL IMPRESSION of the 1960s is that it was a period of female liberation and advance; but talking to Hannah's contemporaries, reading their books, suggests that Hannah's last few years, the early years of the 1960s, were a time of particular, and particularly acute, challenges for women, and especially strong, bright, ambitious women like Hannah.

In the 1950s, things were at least clearer. If a woman wanted a career, she had to sacrifice something. 'It was exhausting to be even moderately "extraordinary" in that decade,' Sheila Rowbotham wrote in a review of Rachel Cooke's *Her Brilliant Career: ten extraordinary women of the Fifties*, and there were 'painful costs'. Such women's 'endeavour isolated them from other women', and if they had children they were 'apt to bundle' them 'off to boarding school'.

An article published in *Historical Research* in 2003 by Elizabeth Kirk, 'Women Academics at Royal Holloway and Bedford Colleges, 1939–69', explores the experiences of the generation before Hannah's.

The article quotes Gertrude Williams, Hannah's original head of department, confessing 'in a sad moment that she had been successful in large because unfortunately she had been unable to have children'. Of the other two senior women sociologists at Bedford in the 1950s, Barbara Wootton was childless, and Marjorie McIntosh, who had three children, 'paid the price of an early death', by stroke in her early fifties. Her death 'sent a clear message to her students: "having it all" (a stressful job and a family) could have fatal consequences'.

As the 1960s progressed, things began to change. More women, helped by the new grants system, were going to university. More jobs were opening up for young women like Anne Wicks in the expanding businesses of the media and advertising. The arrival of the pill meant that women could have sex without worrying about getting pregnant. But while one foot was advancing into a new age, the other was still firmly planted in the 1950s.

These were the days when abortion was illegal, when men filled out their wives' tax forms, when a husband couldn't legally rape his wife. When Jessica Mann, a Cambridge graduate, went to live in Edinburgh with her husband in the early 1960s and applied to the university appointments board for work, she was asked by the man interviewing her, 'What do you want a job for — you're married, aren't you?'

Most of Hannah's contemporaries at Bedford, graduating in 1959 and 1960, went into traditional caring professions, and gave up work when they had children. One did manage to become the first woman on the graduate trainee scheme at Ogilvy & Mather, and went on to have a career in advertising — but she recalls sharing a flat with several women on the Shell graduate-trainee scheme who were in training to be secretaries for their male counterparts.

Sexual behaviour was changing, but sexual attitudes lagged behind. Sheila Rowbotham, who went up to Oxford in 1961, writes in *Promise of a Dream*, her memoir of the 1960s, how a girl she knew was found in bed with a boy. The girl was 'kicked out of college, lost her grant and could not get into any other university'. The boy 'was sent away from his college for two weeks'.

This was still a time when the BBC could send Christopher Brasher to Birmingham University to interview female students for a programme on whether 'women want to compete with men or be competed for by men'.

These mixed messages pervaded married life for women of Hannah's generation. An entry from Phyll Willmott's diary in October 1965, a few weeks before Hannah's death, gives a fascinating glimpse into the dynamics of a 1960s London middle-class marriage. Phyll's husband, Peter ('Petie'), was the breadwinner and a renowned sociologist, but Phyll was herself an expert on the social services — a book she co-edited, *The Social Workers*, was published by Penguin around the time of this entry:

> Petie gave me a little 'pep talk' this morning before going to work! I explained I felt a bit at sea — not sure where I was going from now on, wondering a bit whether I ought to take on more of a 'proper job' with the boys so nearly grown. Feelings of guilt and parasitism etc. Petie, he says, would rather, ideally, I did less not more. He says he wants support from me in carrying his own load of responsibilities and although he likes me to have my own interests and sees I need them, he wants

me not to get more pressed and so on. In other words, he would prefer me to go on much as I have been in the last two years. Free-wheeling away, taking an interest in his work, having my own small 'reputation'. The talk helped.

Hannah was more fortunate in some ways than Phyll, and other women of her age. Her husband's success in his work meant she could afford a full-time nanny, and later an au pair girl, and as long as it didn't interfere with the running of the household, my father encouraged Hannah to study and work.

She was lucky, too, in being naturally strong in will and character. One of Hannah's Bedford contemporaries told me how she went back to the college to do some research on battered babies, but McGregor 'called me in and told me that no one was interested in the subject, and bullied me into giving up'.

Hannah didn't give up. 'She had no sense of deferring to authority,' Bernice Martin said. 'To succeed in those days, women had to give up something — children, work, femininity — whereas Hannah wanted and appeared able to have everything.'

But having everything, as the brave new world of the 1960s seemed perhaps for the first time in history to be offering, wasn't easy. It took a lot of effort, as it does today, to be a mother, a wife, a worker. There was little slack in Hannah's life, Gunilla Lavelle told me. There was no room for spontaneity in how she lived, Erica said. And there was also the not-so-brave old patriarchy waiting to trip up the new woman, belittle her, force her back.

TOWARDS THE END OF 2010, around the time I was having these conversations, I went with my wife to our local cinema to see *Made in Dagenham*. It is based on the true story of the strike for equal pay by the women workers at the Ford car plant in Dagenham in 1968. I thought it might have some relevance to Hannah's story, but that was not our main reason for going. It had been reviewed well, as a British 'feelgood film', so it promised to be a relaxing night out.

The film was chirpy, cheeky, and we were soon laughing with the rest of the audience. ('Chop, chop, or we'll miss the buffet,' one of the young women workers tells her boyfriend as he has sex with her in his car.)

But as the film went on, and though the tone remained mostly light, and the jokes continued to come, my own mood changed. As the women workers — and, in particular, the main character, a young woman who even looked with her dark bob and big smile a little like Hannah — grew in militancy, in determination, they met with increasing condescension, anger, and obstruction from most of the men in the film. Watching the slights the main character received at the hands of a bullying schoolmaster, patronising union leaders and bosses, an initially uncomprehending husband, and even her female friends — let alone having to deal with her own uncertainties — it seemed to me that I was seeing into Hannah's heart, my mother's own struggles, and I watched the last hour with tears running helplessly down my cheeks.

Autumn 1965

A significant change has taken place in the subject matter of the British cinema. In recent years it has been preoccupied with the difficulties of the young working-class male. In these films women were shadowy figures.

In the last six months, however, two films with quite a different subject have appeared. The first of these was *Darling*, whose protagonist is a free woman in the sense that Doris Lessing uses the term. That is a woman who wants to make the same kinds of choices that men can make, and enjoy the same kinds of freedom that men possess. The mistake of the heroine in that film was to think that being a free woman was simply to enjoy sexual freedom, which merely extended the range of her activities but gave no freedom at all.

However a second film has just appeared which can truly be said to be for women, and about women, in the sense that it deals with women's desire to be free, and given both the structure of our society and their own biological and emotional make up, their inability to hold onto that freedom if they get it. This film is *Four in the Morning* which contains three separate sad stories about women, all cleverly woven into one, so that in fact it could be the story of the same girl at different stages of her life. The stories concern one of a pair of would-be lovers who fail to relate, a young married couple whose marriage has become a trap, and the removal from the Thames and the classification at the morgue of a young unidentified woman aged about twenty-six who has committed suicide.

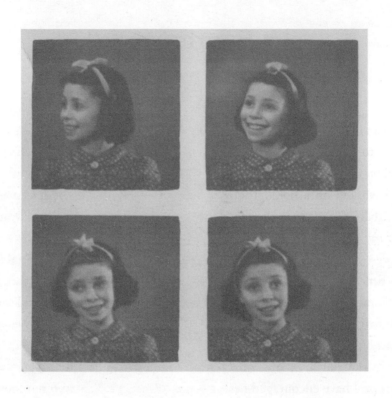

Fourteen

I WAS FIRST CONSCIOUS of suicide as a companion myself when I came back to London at the age of twenty-nine, Hannah's last age. I had broken up with my girlfriend, and was spending a lot of my time alone as I worked on a book. Things I had witnessed as a journalist mixed in my head with thoughts of Hannah, her death, and at night I would lull myself to sleep with images of bullets barrelling towards me, and knives, sometimes held in my own hand, plunging into my chest.

Since then I have never entirely lost these thoughts; I have carried with me, through bad times and good, the possibility of suicide, its comfort, its siren voice. But in all these years I have never seriously considered, or taken any practical steps towards, killing myself.

In the course of my conversations with Hannah's friends, perhaps because I have encouraged them to break one taboo, I have often found myself in the role of confessor, privy to their secret griefs. I have heard stories of rape, marital violence, struggles with alcohol, depression. One woman told me how she had locked herself in the lavatory and taken valium at her own wedding. Another spoke of her fiancé drowning in the Arctic, his body never found.

But for all their troubles, they are all here to talk about them. So why not Hannah? How did her 'ordinary life crisis' carry her to her death?

THERE ARE MANY THEORIES about suicide. For Camus, 'judging whether life is or is not worth living' is 'the fundamental question of philosophy'. For Freud, *thanatos*, or the death drive, is the desire to return to the state of quiescence that precedes birth. For Durkheim, suicide is a product of social forces: either the bonds to the community are too weak, or too strong, or the suicide is caught out by abrupt social change.

I have been given, have read in my grandfather's diaries and elsewhere, more particular explanations for Hannah's suicide. She was depressive. She was narcissistic. She was schizoid. She was ruthless. She burned too brightly to live a whole life. She couldn't bear rejection, imperfection, compromise.

My grandfather seems to have wanted to believe, in his constant returning in his diaries to her childhood dramas, that the 'suicide potential', as Durkheim called it, was inside her all along, though at other times he blamed Anne Wicks, or O. R. McGregor. For a period I was convinced, or tried to convince myself, that the answer lay with the headmaster's abuse — that he was the smoking gun.

But, of course, no suicide is the product of only one thing. In 2004, a new type of verdict, the narrative verdict, was introduced into coroners' courts in England and Wales. Narrative verdicts are used in instances where the cause of death, or the responsibility for that death, cannot be easily categorised: such as the shooting of a man mistakenly identified as a terrorist, or when it is not clear whether a person has meant to take his or her own life.

A narrative verdict wasn't available at Hannah's inquest — and even if it had been, it couldn't have been used. As the coroner said, it was clear that Hannah 'deliberately and efficiently' took her own life. But then the coroner's concern was only with how Hannah died — not why she killed herself.

A narrative verdict is available to me, though. It is not a perfectly formed story. It may be partly questions or lists. It may present opposing ideas. It accepts that it doesn't provide a complete or unchallengeable account. It is as much as is known, as much as can be drawn from the information available.

What follows is my narrative verdict, my attempt to fathom what Hannah's coroner described as 'a state of mind we cannot know'.

'WE WERE TOO YOUNG to get married,' my father admitted in one of our talks. But he was twenty-four, nearly twenty-five. Since leaving school seven years earlier, he had completed his national service in the army, partly in Berlin during the airlift, a time he talks about fondly. He was twice made corporal, and twice busted down to private. He rode a motorbike, made a parachute jump, had a German girlfriend, was taught to foxtrot and quickstep by the sergeant-major's wife.

After the army, he went to Oxford, where he performed in comedy sketches, played rugby and cricket for his college, edited the books pages of the university newspaper. He had a serious affair with a girl he thought about marrying. He earned a law degree. He made friends and connections to last a lifetime.

After Oxford, he spent a year teaching at a boarding school, where he had his passionate liaison with the under matron. He passed his bar exams. By the time of his marriage, he had been working at his cousin-in-law's printing company for a year and a half and been promoted to sales director, on a good salary.

He was young for the job, but he wanted what came with being older, with success, with being established. When, not long after, he was made managing director of the company, he went to a barber and asked for a haircut to make him look older. The barber suggested dying his sideburns grey, and as a result the secretaries 'treated him more seriously'. He was too embarrassed to do it again, but he took up smoking cigars to give himself gravitas.

'I was anxious to get on,' he told an interviewer on a BBC radio Home Service programme in November 1963. He was also happy to be married, settled. He adored Hannah, and wanted children. 'I never wanted to be anything other than a family man,' Phyll Willmott remembers him telling her after Hannah's death.

HANNAH, TOO, had always wanted to be older, was impatient to grow up. She insisted on leaving school before she had completed her A levels. She wanted to be married at seventeen, my grandmother's story went, and I can believe that, like some of the women she wrote about in *The Captive Wife*, she was 'desperate' to leave home, to escape the constrictions of living with her parents.

But for all her precocity, her veneer of sophistication, her letters show how young she still was. The way she writes of the 'utter heaven' of driving my father's car. Her excitement at telling Tasha about my father sleeping in her bed 'all night'. Was this the first time she had spent a night in bed with a man?

Her letters also reveal her nervousness at the speed at which things were advancing with my father. In the first letter that mentions him, he is already asking her 'to come and live with him (I declined)' and within two months he has given her 'an open offer of marriage'. She is 'scared', she writes.

She was eighteen when she married. Her application for a new passport in her married name for her honeymoon tells its own story. In the first page (the rest is missing) of a letter to Tasha, she writes, 'we had a simply heavenly honey moon encountering none of the traditional difficulties'.

But a letter in her RADA file from four months later hints at a realisation that married life might not have been all 'heaven'. 'The end of the year production,' she wrote to the RADA office, 'will be mainly members of my old class and I would love to be able to see them all again on stage, so I wonder if you could possibly let me have two tickets.' Was she regretting, in some part of her, leaving RADA so hurriedly, swapping its excitement and companionship for ironing shirts, cooking meals, waiting for her husband to come home? 'I do expect an occasional letter,' she wrote to Tasha, who was now at Oxford University, 'if only to describe to me the life I have somehow managed to miss.'

THESE FEELINGS DO NOT SEEM to have been too long lasting or serious at this stage. She was young, life lay ahead of her, nothing was too serious. She was in love with my father, had the excitement of holidays in the south of France and the Alps, weekends at hotels by the sea. She was soon, anyway, taking up a place at university herself, and if any doubts, regrets, rose up in the years ahead — when she found herself a mother at twenty-one and again at twenty-four, in her interviews with her captive wives, at dinners with my father's middle-aged business associates — her days were too full of her children, her studies, attending to my father, running the household, to dwell on them.

The change came, or began to come, when she went to work at Hornsey College of Art. Her first year seems to have been a time of settling in, learning how to handle a class, give a lecture. She was still working hard on her thesis, and a good deal of her energy was also going into supporting my father in his efforts to buy his own printing company. In one of the notes to my father, I found in my stepmother's filing cabinet, Hannah wrote how she 'put myself to one side and threw myself completely into helping you get what you wanted'.

But by the time she started her second year at Hornsey, in

September 1964, my father's business deal had been secured, and he was concentrating on turning around his new company, with fewer demands on Hannah. She had completed her thesis, and was waiting for it to be approved. Simon was at school, and at three I had also now started at full-time nursery. For the first time, perhaps, since Simon was born, every minute of her day was not prescribed.

Hornsey was itself going through a period of rapid change as it embraced, helped to create, the new mood and ideas of the 1960s. 'Many of the era's distinctive cultural developments' sprang from the art colleges, Brian Marwick, a historian of the 1960s, wrote in the *Sunday Times*. 'At Salford, Hornsey, Norwich and St Martins,' they discussed 'Sartre, played rock'n'roll and designed clothes'.

More younger teachers were being taken on for the expanding general studies course, including, in September 1964, John Hayes. A month later, on 11 October, my grandfather noted in his diary that Hannah had changed: 'Exotic looking: black hair straightened, red dress, brown skin.'

MOST OF MY PARENTS' FRIENDS, their neighbours, my father himself, were forward-thinking for their time, were the generation who had laid the groundwork for the 1960s. But they were already in their thirties, even forties, when it came along: the 1960s, as Larkin famously wrote, were 'just too late' for them.

Hannah, though, was those few years younger, still on the right side of thirty. She was spending her days at Hornsey, mixing with younger people, teaching young artists, watching them enjoy the fruits, the sexual intercourse, and 'unlosable game', as Larkin put it, of the unfolding new age. She had also spent the last year writing up her interviews with young mothers who lamented that they had given up their youth too soon. 'I'd like to have had more time for going dancing,' one told her; 'I would have liked to have travelled,' said another.

Among the papers from my stepmother's filing cabinet is a page torn out of a women's magazine. Part of a feature on 'The '64 Beat', it shows a young woman with the Mary Quant bob that Hannah adopted that autumn — or the 'Boop-Boop-a-Do', as the magazine called it. Dressing up in a new way, Angela Carter wrote in a 1967 essay, 'Notes for a Theory of Sixties Style', 'gives a relaxation from one's own personality and the discovery of maybe unsuspected new selves'. Clad in her red dress, or her mini skirt, and thigh-length Courrèges boots, with her Boop-Boop-a-Doo hairstyle, Hannah was a new person, newly young. She stood in the corridors at Hornsey, as David Page remembers, smoking her cheroots, eyeing up the male students. And, in time, as young people do, she fell in love.

THE WAY JOHN HAYES describes his relationship with Hannah — the excitable talk, the exploration of sexuality — makes it sound like a university love affair, and perhaps that was what it was like for Hannah, too, at first. More than one person has told me how attractive John was, with his wavy blonde hair and northern charm. There was the thrill of discovering someone new, the illicit assignations. Their school days, Hannah had written to Tasha, had left them with the feeling that 'if one is not in love with anyone in particular, life is very dreary'.

But if the affair began as a reclamation of her too quickly abandoned youth, a facing down of regrets, it soon seems to have grown, at least for Hannah, into something more serious, more freighted. It was partly that her situation was less carefree than John's. She had children. She didn't have an understanding with my father about affairs, as John had with the other John. But being with John also opened Hannah's eyes to new possibilities, to a new kind of relationship for a new kind of woman in the new world.

My sense is that my father hadn't changed much in the years of their marriage. He had become more successful, more confident, had grown more into himself. But Hannah at twenty-nine was very different from the clever schoolgirl with dreams of being an actress she had been when she met my father. She had experienced the realities of married life, motherhood. She had spent several years studying the situation of young women in society. Working at Hornsey had exposed her to new ways of thinking. Nina Kidron told me that her husband, Michael, a Marxist thinker and colleague of Hannah's at Hornsey, had 'radicalised Hannah, introduced her to left-wing ideas'. Susie, too, remembers a rare conversation in Hannah's last summer in which she confided that a 'world was opening up for her because of her job at Hornsey, that she was meeting interesting new people with radical views, and was finding herself in tune with these views, not just in sociology, but in philosophy, politics, design, psychology'.

My father was unusual for a businessman. He was a Labour voter and a voracious reader. But his natural affinity was more for Dickens than Saul Bellow, whose novels Susie says Hannah liked; more for Rossetti than the op-artist Vasarely Susie remembers as Hannah's favourite; more for classical music than the Beatles songs Hannah sung while straddling the front of the boat in France; more for Darwinian ideas of the survival of the fittest than the psychedelic psychiatry of R. D. Laing, who, I know from Tasha, Hannah 'greatly admired'.

Hannah was no shrinking housewife, but the difference in my parents' ages when they met, and the early years of their marriage, when my father was markedly more advanced in life, had laid down an imbalance of power that was reinforced by his success as a pugnacious entrepreneur ('One has to be aggressive,' he told the interviewer on the 1963 BBC radio programme. 'One has to attack.') and his control of the purse strings. One of Hannah's contemporaries at Bedford told me a story about Hannah coming into college with lipstick on and explaining that she was wearing it because she had a tan from skiing. Her husband, she said, did not like her to wear make-up unless she had a tan.

It was the way of the times. 'The idea that in marriage the wife should submerge herself in her husband still persists,' Hannah wrote in *The Captive Wife*. Another strong woman, Sheila Rowbotham, wrote of her reasons for breaking up with an older man she loved in the 1960s. 'In some confused sense I intimated that I could not become myself because I was always in [his] shadow ... I could not find an independent track while remaining connected to him.'

But it was a way that Hannah, in *The Captive Wife*, in how she was trying to live, was challenging; a way that she felt could be different with John. 'There will always be a part of me that you made and which belongs to you,' she wrote in one of her notes to my father in those last weeks. 'But you need the kind of person I cannot be.' To my grandfather, she was more dramatic. Hannah 'fighting for her identity as an individual', he recorded in his diary.

IN OCTOBER 1965, under pressure to see a psychiatrist, Hannah travelled to Sussex University to talk to her GP friend Tony Ryle. Tony wasn't a psychiatrist, but he was a doctor with a growing interest in psychotherapy.

Nearly half a century later, I follow Hannah down to Sussex, where Tony Ryle still lives. His memories of Hannah's visit are still clear in his mind. She came to see him 'in distress', he says. She had been 'under a lot of pressure for a long time'. Connecting 'femininity, intellectual and family life was not easy'. To find the space to get a first-class degree and a PhD, while having two children, running a household, and looking after my father, had 'taken a lot out of her'. The title of her book 'wasn't an accident'.

His reading of her affair with John Hayes is that she was seeking 'the other side of the coin'. My father was a 'strong, determined older male figure who didn't like being challenged', while John was her own age, 'more gentle and sensitive'. John's homosexuality was part of the attraction to Hannah. She could 'introduce him to heterosexual sex, be the dominant partner, in charge of the relationship'. Society at that time 'preprogrammed women to accept a life structure of powerful men and subservient women, but in the end Hannah rebelled against this'. She was 'discomforted with herself, and her affair with John Hayes was an attempt to find comfort, to find ease in herself.

JOHN HAYES WAS ULTIMATELY 'a false solution' for Hannah, Tony Ryle suggests. In affairs, people 'often go for someone who supplies the parts they don't get from their marriage, rather than the whole person'. But if Tony said this to Hannah in 1965, she doesn't seem to have agreed. 'I do know that there are very very few men who could be married to a person like me,' she wrote to my father, and John, she appears to have decided, was one of those men.

But as this idea took on more substance in Hannah's mind and she began talking about marriage, living together, John pulled back with equal force, leading to their argument. Exactly how the last acts played out is not entirely clear, though it happened very fast. John suggested the argument might have been on the morning of her death, though the day before seems more likely, for after Hannah's visit that last evening my grandfather wrote of my father having 'a chance', that 'there is no other man on the scene'.

If that was what Hannah told her father, John remembers her telling him that she would be at Anne Wick's flat if he changed his mind. Perhaps this is what Sonia meant by Hannah expecting someone to find her, that it was John she was expecting — though once she

244

had turned on the gas taps, he would have had to arrive within a very narrow window of time to find her still alive. More likely she waited for a while, and when John didn't appear, went ahead with her plan.

She was 'cheerful' the previous evening, my grandfather wrote, and even on her last morning she was in 'a good mood', according to Jeanie. If this suggests that the idea wasn't yet in her mind, the half bottle of vodka is evidence otherwise, and the good mood could have another explanation.

People who have survived serious suicide attempts sometimes speak of a feeling of relief, even euphoria, once the decision is made. A kind of fugue state settles on them, in which nothing matters but the task in hand. The vodka is ordered, the au pair girl is instructed to collect the son. The evidence of Hannah's note — the small envelope, the sparse message, the wild writing that indicates she was already drunk, or perhaps affected by sleeping pills, when she wrote it — suggests that even saying goodbye was an afterthought. 'Please tell the boys I did love them terribly!' she wrote, in the past tense, as if the world had already receded, or she had already receded from the world.

HOW HAD IT come so suddenly to this? Hannah, who was so engaged with the world. Who only a week earlier was planning a new life with John, modern, sexually liberated, equal, uncaptive. The argument with John was the trigger, the sudden bursting of these hopes and plans, but I have come to see that there were other pressures building on her in the last year or two of her life, the last months:

1. HER PARENTS. Though they loved her, wanted the best for her, my grandfather's diaries suggest that from the moment Hannah told them about her affair, they were overwhelmed by their own fears and anxieties.

'Where are my hopes?' my grandfather, ever the Grublergeist, wrote. My grandmother was 'depressed'. They worried about my brother and me: 'neglect must begin'. They worried about my father: 'should have done more for Pop'.

Hannah, with her 'lunatic driving', 'unrepentant', my grandfather called her at one point, was the cause of all this. They pressed her to give up John Hayes, to try again with my father. 'Enormously relieved,' my grandfather wrote when she agreed. 'Not bearable,' when she changed her mind.

They also pressured her to see a psychiatrist, as if her unhappiness in her marriage, her falling in love with another man, her desire to fulfil herself as a woman, were symptoms of mental illness. 'It could be that I am sick,' Hannah wrote sadly in one of her notes to my father. 'Tho I do not think so.'

By the time it occurred to my grandfather that the most troubled person was his daughter, that she might have needed support rather than criticism from her parents, it was too late. 'I should have said to H bring John to see me,' my grandfather lamented in his diary four days after her death. 'I'm good with young men. Should have helped her. In my blindness, my fear of losing Pop, I did not.'

2. WORK. The troubles with her doctorate, the LSE, McGregor, had hit her confidence. And it was only not only her confidence. Bedford and the LSE were the only London University colleges with sociology departments. Even if there had been a job at Sussex, or somewhere else outside London, with two young children it would have been difficult for her to move.

For someone normally so organised and reliable, it is revealing that she seems to have abandoned the introduction to sociology she had signed a contract to write. 'If you can let me have a note of its progress

246

and a likely date of delivery,' her editor wrote to her a few weeks before her death. But when my grandfather went through her work papers later, he found only rough notes for it.

Even the book she had finished, *The Captive Wife*, gave her little cause for optimism. It had been held back by the delay over her thesis, and her desire to see it out by Christmas had been thwarted. Her closest female friend warned her that publishing it would ruin her career. David Page remembers her talking 'disparagingly' about the book, 'something to the effect of "They wanted statistics, so I cobbled some together."' He suggested this showed she didn't care about 'professional cachet', but perhaps it showed how low her confidence was.

In the last couple of weeks she did finally secure a job, at the Institute of Education. It was a good position, but not the academic teaching post she wanted, and too late perhaps, her mind already turned against academics. A year after her death, my grandfather wrote of her asking after her dinner with her prospective employees, 'are BBC people as bitchy as academics?'

3. CHARACTER FLAWS (A). Hannah's life had not prepared her for failure, rejection, disapprobation, shame. The stories my grandmother told about her successes as a poet, rider, actress, woman were understandably exaggerated, but over the course of her twenty-nine years she had usually got what she wanted, succeeded in most of what she did.

She hadn't inherited the family propensities for gloominess, depression, but she does seem to have been prone to anxiety, panic, sudden 'fits of despair', as Sonia described them, on the rare occasions when things did go wrong. Sonia remembered 'floods of tears' if she lost at riding. Susan Downes described Hannah 'turning green and shaking' on the mountain with the headmaster, and again in a classroom with a teacher. In his diary, my grandfather kept coming back to these moments of 'uncontrolled emotions', such as a young Hannah 'standing still and screaming in panic' when cornered in a game of chase with Sonia and Tasha. 'No way out?' he wrote.

Was this how it was with Hannah in those last hours? Did the pressure my grandparents put on her to stop seeing John, to stop being so egotistical, to see a psychiatrist, take her back to her teenage years, when her escape was to go to boarding school, to marry my father? Where was her way out now?

4. FRIENDS. For most of her life, when she had her despairs, there was someone there to comfort her. Sonia and Tasha would 'calm her down'. Susan Downes acted as the 'big sister type' she needed. My father told me how Hannah would get suddenly upset about something, and he would put his 'arm around her sympathetically and crack a joke, and it would flare down'.

But my father wasn't around in those last weeks and days — she had kicked him out of the house. And where were the close female friends she had relied on in the past? She had started seeing Susan again, but as a couple, without the old closeness, and she saw little in her last years of Shirley, Sonia, even Tasha.

It was partly that they all had their own busy lives. But it was also that Hannah's rush to grow up had pushed her in advance of her old friends. 'Why do I never see or hear from you?' she wrote to Tasha, who was still at school when Hannah got engaged to my father. 'Is it because Pop is a businessman?'

It was partly, too, that her ambitions, her efforts to be a new kind of woman, had isolated her from other women, as it had with the exceptional women in Rachel Cooke's book about the 1950s. Phyll Willmott, a newer friend, but warm, intelligent, living close by, might have been someone who could have provided support and perspective. Phyll even picked up that Hannah 'was having a bad time in some way' and 'wondered if she might talk about it', but when she didn't, Phyll didn't encourage her. After Hannah's death, she wrote of her guilt that she didn't realise that Hannah was in trouble, didn't help her, 'and more guilt because of my always slightly ambivalent feelings towards her'.

It was also, perhaps, her pride, as Gunilla Lavelle said, a reluctance to admit she was in trouble. Hannah was the one advising Tasha with her boyfriend problems, helping Erica with her abortion, climbing through Katrin Stroh's window. She 'always seemed so much in command of every situation it never occurred to us she had problems of her own', Sonia wrote after her death.

The one female friend she did confide in, who knew about John, who allowed her to meet him in her flat, was Anne Wicks. But Anne was another clever, strong, ambitious woman, not the arm-around-the shoulder type. When Hannah told her she would kill herself if John Hayes rejected her, Anne didn't take it seriously. Instead she told Hannah that her book wasn't rigorous enough, that publishing it would ruin her reputation.

5. CHARACTER FLAWS (B). One of the old family friends who I discover goes back to Hannah's time is the playwright Arnold Wesker. 'Her death affected me very deeply,' he writes after I leave a message. 'Not because we knew her intimately but because she was sweet, kind, and beautiful, and her death was so unexpected — she was so young. It affected me so much that I recreated her in one of my stories, "Six Sundays in January". I can't put my hand on my heart and say Katerina Levinson is a head-on portrait of your mother, but something of her atmosphere touches the story. It might give you a hint of her.'

Katerina is not the main character of 'Six Sundays in January'.

The story follows another young mother across a series of Sundays, on one of which she encounters Katerina in a café in the East End. The Sunday afterwards, the phone rings with the news that Katerina has killed herself.

It is not a head-on portrait, Arnold writes; he didn't know Hannah well. But he knew her a little, knew the times, knew women of her age struggling perhaps with similar things, was an intuitive witness to the world he was living in.

Sheila Rowbotham, writing of her own struggles as a young woman in the 1960s, used remarkably similar language as Arnold to describe her own 'splintering identity, seeking words that somehow glance off my fingertips, clinging to an assortment of stray ends I couldn't fit together'. There is something, too, in Katerina's monologues of Hannah's sweeping dismissals of her contemporaries to her grandfather: 'The young technicians are too busy acquiring their little car.'

Was this Hannah in her last days? Frail, battered, splintered. Oversensitive to fraudulence (those 'bitchy' academics). Despairing of the 'facile image' of women that 'countless magazines perpetrate'. Bruised by her own young man with his 'pleasant songs' who had disappeared and left 'great confusion'.

'I don't want any more knowledge of pain,' Katerina says. 'Forgive me Annie,' Hannah wrote on the envelope. 'But the pain was too much.'

Another woman might have struggled on, accepted compromises, confided in friends, waited for things to get better, the winter to turn into spring, her book to be published. But Hannah wasn't much good at patience, compromise, asking for help. In her nature was rather a family unreadiness to be taken beyond a certain limit, an accompanying steeliness, ruthlessness. A disregard, too, for the usual

250

rules, the accepted codes, of life. 'The whole of that terrific force,' my psychoanalyst neighbour said, 'turned against herself'.

IN SOME WAYS, I am the least qualified person to write about Hannah. Unlike the people I have interviewed about her, I have no memories of my own of her. But, at the same time, I am her son. Half the genes that shaped me I got from her. If I didn't know her, I knew her parents, her other son, know her sister, her five grandchildren. If the Hannah of these pages is a construct of other people's memories, viewpoints, and my own imagination, then that imagination is informed by the knowledge, the instinctive connection, that blood brings.

I have come, I feel, to understand her. I get her sense of humour. That she could be both selfish and generous, both emotional and rational, makes sense to me. I understand her irreverence, her outrageousness, her melodramas, her moral integrity, her sense of justice. I understand her when she is difficult.

I even feel that I understand her suicide, or at least the steps that led to her suicide — except for one key element of the story: how she came to invest herself so completely in a future with John Hayes that was so clearly a fantasy, a 'fiction', as my grandfather's friend said.

We all make mistakes, see things wrongly, at times. Hannah was known when she was younger for imagining dull romances into great love affairs. But that was when she was a teenager. The Hannah who so misjudged what was happening with John Hayes was a woman of nearly thirty, with two children, ten years of marriage behind her. She was the Hannah who had navigated her controversial doctorate through hostile waters to the verge of publication, the author of the clear-eyed prose of *The Captive Wife*. The woman John Hayes himself described as having an 'intense clarity of mind that burned like a sun'.

It wasn't that John wasn't worth wanting a future with. He was

251

handsome, intelligent, charming, a grammar-school boy who had made his way to Oxford. He would go on to have sparkling friendships with brilliant women like Angela Carter and Carmen Callil, as he might have had with Hannah under different circumstances.

It wasn't even, or only, that he was homosexual, that he had never slept with a woman before Hannah. He wouldn't have been the first person to discover new elements of sexuality in a love affair. But while Hannah and my father had separated, and Hannah was talking about divorce, John Hayes was still firmly living with the other John, as he still does today. When Hannah mentioned marriage, moving in together, John had 'a major recoil'. Their few sexual encounters had been 'tawdry', a 'mistake'. He had never met Simon and me, let alone entertained the idea of becoming our stepfather. And suddenly, out of nowhere, Hannah was talking about being married by Christmas.

Love can be blinding. Cherry Marshall told my grandfather how, when she had fallen in love with a man outside her marriage, 'husband, children, work — all vanished. It was like catching a disease.' But for it to be so deluding to such an intelligent woman, such an acute observer of other people, someone who had managed her own life so successfully — it was as if she had lost her wits, lost her mind.

I GO BACK OVER MY NOTES, searching for an explanation. Anne Wicks told my grandfather that Hannah was worried she would be 'an old maid if John did not marry her', and was 'genuinely afraid of being alone'. Can this be the answer? Did she really think that John Hayes was her last chance?

It seems a ridiculous thing for a beautiful, intelligent, twenty-nine-year-old woman to believe. But is that a twenty-first century perspective? In my efforts to understand Hannah, I have been reading writing by women of her time. The great woman's novel of Hannah's last years was Doris Lessing's *The Golden Notebook*, published in 1962. It is a sacred feminist work, a 'powerful account of a woman searching for her personal and political identity', as it says on the back of my paperback copy. But veined through the novel, for character after character, even those who are trying most forcefully to be 'free women', is the question of whether a woman can be happy without a man.

'Women's emotions are all still fitted for a kind of society that no longer exists,' says Ella, a fictional woman within the fiction. 'My deep emotions, my real ones are to do with my relationship with a man.' Even the novel's protagonist, Anna Wulf, confesses, 'I'd like to be married. I don't like living like this.' To be with a man is 'to cancel myself out', but to be without a man is to be 'alone, frightened to be alone, without resources'.

Memoirs of real free women of the period tell of similar fears. Sheila Rowbotham writes that she 'could not become myself' while living in her boyfriend's shadow, but when she left him she found herself 'unsure how to be apart and on my own. A diffuse anxiety assumed physical form one night when I was overwhelmed by a choking feeling which left me panting for breath.'

Even Joan Bakewell, the epitome of the woman who had it all, came to a crisis when her marriage fell apart. 'I found myself alone with two young children to care for,' she writes in *The Centre of the Bed*. 'Emotionally I was confused and unhappy, drifting deeper and deeper into bewilderment and despair.'

I AM TRYING to make sense of this when the latest edition of the *New Yorker* magazine drops through my letterbox. Inside is an article by Susan Faludi about an American feminist who recently died. 'Death of a Revolutionary', it is headlined. 'Shulamith Firestone helped to create a new society. But she couldn't live in it.'

253

I am immediately struck by similarities between Shulamith Firestone and Hannah. Fiery and stubborn, Firestone skipped the last year of school to get away from her Jewish parents and train to be a painter. She published an early feminist text. She was both striking looking — 'a mane of black hair down to her waist, and piercing dark eyes' — and charismatic. 'It was thrilling to be in her company,' one friend is quoted as saying. 'She flashed brightly across the midnight sky,' another said at her funeral, 'and then she disappeared.'

As I read on, the two stories separate. Firestone never married, had no children. She was almost a decade younger than Hannah, and far more radical. She also developed schizophrenia. Not long after her book was published, she withdrew from the feminist scene, and in time withdrew from life. She became an eccentric, wandering her neighbourhood in New York. She was hospitalised several times and died alone in an East Village tenement walk-up.

This was not Hannah. But the article goes on to consider the 'whole generation' of founding American feminists, how so many of them were 'unable to thrive in the world they had done so much to create'. As well as Firestone, there was Kate Millett, who had a breakdown and was hospitalised after publishing the best-selling *Sexual Politics*, also in 1970, and others who ended in 'painful solitude, poverty, infirmity', and in two named cases, suicide.

The article quotes another early feminist, Meredith Tax, who used the phrase 'female schizophrenia' to describe 'a realm of unreality where a woman either belonged to a man or was "nowhere, disappeared, teetering on the edge of a void"'. It also refers to Elaine Showalter's book, *The Female Malady*, about women and madness in England, and I look this up. Showalter's main thesis is that female madness is a construction of male society, that when women challenge the status quo they are told they are mad (as Hannah was pressed to see a psychiatrist when she fell in love with another man.) But Showalter also suggests that women's position in a man's world can actually drive them mad.

Her chapter on the 1960s focuses on R. D. Laing, the Scottish 'anti-psychiatrist' Hannah admired. The book Hannah probably read was his 1960 work, *The Divided Self*, which argues that schizophrenia in women isn't an illness but a response to an 'unlivable situation'. With her nature in conflict with her environment, a woman is 'split in two'.

Could this be the explanation? That Hannah was schizoid after all? That she was driven mad, split in two, by the conflict of her situation?

Among the papers from my stepmother's filing cabinet is a rough draft of a review Hannah wrote of two films. It is unfinished, and I haven't been able to discover whether it was ever published. It is also undated, but the films were released in mid-1965, so it must have been written in her last months.

Darling, starring Julie Christie and Dirk Bogarde, is a glamorous 1960s tragedy about a woman who gorges on the fruits of her beauty but then finds herself alone, and in desperation agrees to a loveless marriage. *Four in the Morning* is smaller, more sombre, offering little hope for female fulfillment and happiness in the modern world, and ends, as Hannah wrote, with the body of an 'unidentified young woman aged about twenty six who has committed suicide'.

Other than her returned cheques, these are Hannah's last surviving written words.

THE FILMS, Hannah's review, address the dilemma of modern women's 'desire to be free, and given both the structure of our society and their own biological and emotional make up, their inability to hold onto that freedom'. But Hannah wasn't only trying to live as a free woman. She was, like the early American feminists, immersed in the subject

255

intellectually. She had devoted much of the last years of her life to talking to captive wives, to thinking, researching, and writing about ways to free such women from that captivity.

As much, perhaps, as any other woman in England at the time, Hannah had a clear view of what was wrong with the world from a woman's point of view, what needed to be changed, and had experienced, too, in her work the difficulties of challenging the status quo. Victorian women pioneers 'could still make a fuss and change things the way we can't any more', she told my grandfather. 'Intellectuals are no use to anybody today.'

'There are no easy answers to the question of how you live in a world you want to change radically,' Sheila Rowbotham wrote. If Hannah had been a few years younger, writing a few years later, she would have come across women like Rowbotham, Juliet Mitchell, Germaine Greer. In the last months of the 1960s, the first women's groups began to appear, offering support to women trying to change things in the world, in their own lives. But those few years earlier, Hannah in her work, and in a life informed by that work, was very much alone.

Whether because she was mad in those last days, or the world was mad, she put everything into her relationship with John Hayes, into the brave new life she imagined with him, because she had to — because, once she had seen a different way of being, she could not accept living by the old ways. 'We were like pioneers who'd left the Old Country,' another early feminist told Susan Faludi. 'And we had nowhere to go back to.' 'When it didn't work out with John Hayes,' Tony Ryle told me, 'she couldn't go back and she couldn't go forward.'

I grew up with the idea of there being two Hannahs: the Hannah who wanted everything out of life, and the Hannah who wanted nothing. Perhaps this was because her 'unlivable situation' split her 'in two'. Or perhaps there is another way to think about it. That she died not despite the life force, the character, that her friends remember, that won her showjumping cups, led her to marry at eighteen, to write *The Captive Wife*, but because of it.

This be one more fact

BUT OF COURSE no narrative, no narrative verdict, is ever really complete. In one last conversation about Hannah, my father mentions that he thinks she had another affair before the one with John Hayes. He has told me this before, I realise, but I hadn't really taken it in — perhaps because I wasn't sure whether to believe him, perhaps because I wasn't ready to hear it myself.

'With who?' I say now, thinking he will take it back, or tell me he doesn't know, doesn't remember.

'A doctor.'

'What doctor?'

'You don't know him.'

'What was his name?'

He purses his lips. 'Why do you want to know?'

'I'm interested.'

'John Paulett,' he says, eventually.

He and Hannah met John Paulett and his wife on a beach in the south of France, he says. The Pauletts lived in Bexleyheath. Hannah was 'always keen to visit them there'.

'How do you know they were having an affair?'

'I don't,' he says. 'But I suspected.'

'What made you suspect?'

'I was sitting on the sofa with the wife, and she tried to make up to me, and when I protested, she asked me what I thought the others were doing in the next room.'

He hadn't thought anything of it at the time. He was naive, he thought the wife was just a bit strange, but afterwards —

His voice trails off; he has said more than he intended.

'When was this?' I ask.

'Oh, quite a lot earlier.'

'How much earlier?'

'The late Fifties.'

'But that was before I was born,' I protest.

'Yes,' he says firmly. 'Between Simon and you.'

JOHN PAULETT, I discover online, was born in 1918 — he was twelve years older than my father, eighteen older than Hannah — and died in 1997. He had three wives and two children. One of the children is called Daphne, and I find a Daphne Paulett in Greece. She has an email address, and I send her a brief email saying that I think her father might have known my mother.

'Yes, John Paulett was my dad,' she replies, 'and I do remember your mother. Please ask me what you want to know.'

I write back a careful email, suggesting only that her father may have had some influence on Hannah. I don't want to be the one to tell her about her father and my mother, or to claim something that is not true.

But she writes back, 'I am pretty sure that my dad had an affair with Hannah.'

They lived in St Paul's Cray, not Bexleyheath, she says. She remembers my parents visiting: 'a couple who used to live in London who would bring us strange things from the city, like avocado pears'.

This sounds right — my uncle used to send boxes of avocados from Israel.

In further emails, she tells me a little more. Her father was 'a strong influence on everybody that knew him'. Her mother also killed herself, in 1963, when Daphne was twelve — after 'a very huge fight with my dad'. Daphne found her.

Her father wrote a book called *Neurosis*. He had lots of affairs. Her mother's death was several years after his affair with Hannah, she assures me — was nothing to do with that.

She sends me a photograph of him: a good-looking man in a white shirt, collar turned up, sleeves rolled, standing in his garden holding up a fox he had killed, she writes, because it invaded his chicken run. Three dead chickens also lie at his feet.

I AM STUNNED by all this. I thought I had understood Hannah, had made sense of her life and death — and now this changes everything. John Paulett wasn't the 'other side of the coin', as Tony Ryle had said of John Hayes, but another powerful older man.

I spend more time at the computer, and learn that he was a political radical, one of the original Committee of a Hundred, the anti-war group set up to demonstrate against nuclear weapons in 1960, along with Ralph Miliband, Arnold Wesker, Lindsay Anderson, John Osborne, and others.

How do I reconcile this with my theories about Hannah's need to be young again, to free herself from male domination, that it was at Hornsey that she was radicalised?

BETWEEN SIMON AND ME, my father insisted. Before I was born. My God, I think for a minute, John Paulett could be my father — before reason returns to me. I only have to look in the mirror to know who my father is.

My father, who is not usually good on dates, was surprisingly sure about when this affair happened. What could have fixed the time in his mind? I think of his spine operation — how he was on his back in hospital for six weeks in 1959. He made a point of telling me how good Hannah was to him then, how she was at his bedside every day — but perhaps she was being so nice to make up for what she was doing when she wasn't there.

I remember also about Hannah's miscarriage between Simon and me. I am not John Paulett's son — but could the miscarried baby have been? Was this what Hannah's story of the two-headed baby was about? A baby with two heads because it had two fathers — because she didn't know which one was the father?

FOR THE FIRST TIME in my life, I am angry with Hannah. I think of David Page's description of her fancying male students. I have loved this image ever since I got the letter — this ballsy, Mae West-ish Hannah. But now there is something disturbing about it. Who else was she sleeping with?

There is something sickening, too, about the thought that she was having an affair before I was born. Why bring a child into an already fractured family?

THOUGH, AS TIME PASSES, my anger fades. It is hard to be angry with someone for giving me life. It is hard to be angry with someone whose own life was so foreshortened — who missed out on so much.

She would be in her seventies now, if she had lived — a grey-haired grandmother of five. In all the years since, I have only ever had one dream in which she appeared. It was shortly after I had come back to London from my years abroad. I was her last age, though in my dream she was middle-aged, motherly, even a little plump.

I don't remember her saying anything, only sitting at the end of my bed, as if I had woken from sleep to find her there. I remember how happy I felt in my dream — and that the happiness stayed with me for days.

I SET OUT on these inquiries as a son looking for a mother — but the Hannah I have found is not that motherly, middle-aged woman, or the woman in her seventies she would be now. She is the Hannah of her childhood, her teens, her twenties. The Hannah who will never grow older than twenty-nine. I am fifty-two as I write the final version of these last words, the years between us almost the same as they were when I was born, though I am now the older, old enough to be her father.

I have done what I can to give Hannah life again, in my head, on these pages, as a father gives life to a daughter. Now, as a father must eventually let go of his daughters, as I have already begun to do with my own daughters as they grow towards adulthood, I must let my mother go.

Acknowledgements

The suicide doesn't go alone, he takes everybody with him.
William Maxwell

This is not my book alone. It could not have been written without the contributions of my father, my aunt, my stepmother, and other members of my family, and of Hannah's friends and colleagues, who so generously dug up old memories, photographs, diaries, letters. Some are mentioned in these pages; others, not. I owe a great debt of gratitude to all of them.

Carmen Callil and Joan Aleshire read earlier drafts and gave invaluable advice. Clare Alexander, wise and never wavering, did the same and much more. Philip Gwyn Jones, Molly Slight, Sarah Braybrooke, and Henry Rosenbloom guided me on the final steps.

Henry Singer gave friendship.

Rafi Gavron responded from the heart.

Leah and Mima Gavron grew up with this book and never complained, always understood. Leah helped me see the ending.

Judy Henry helped me see. In you I do.